EVIL
ARCHAEOLOGY

EVIL

ARCHAEOLOGY

Demons, Possessions, and Sinister Relics

HEATHER LYNN, PhD

disinformation®

Published by Disinformation Books,
an imprint of Red Wheel/Weiser, LLC
with offices at
65 Parker Street, Suite 7
Newburyport, MA 01950
www.redwheelweiser.com

Library of Congress Cataloging-in-Publication
Data available upon request

Cover design by Kathryn Sky-Peck
Cover illustration © Christopher Leonas
Interior by Steve Amarillo/Urban Design llc
Typeset in Noto Serif/Sans and Emigre Mrs. Eaves

Printed in Canada
MAR

10 9 8 7 6 5 4 3

For those who fear what isn't known,
let light reveal what isn't shown.

Contents

Acknowledgments

I would first like to thank everyone at Red Wheel Weiser, especially my editor for Disinformation Books, Michael Pye. I would also like to thank my amazingly talented artist, Christopher Leonas, for painting the Pazuzu amulet featured on the cover. Thank you to Heidi Stevens, for all your help and support. To my assistant, Tom: thank you for your dedication and enthusiasm. Thank you to Peter Jacobson, who has always been so helpful and encouraging. Thank you to Mike Ricksecker and Bill Bean for your thoughtful contributions. Thank you also to Hakan Ogun. Above all, thank you to my readers for allowing me to explore subjects and ideas that challenge people to look beyond the established historical narrative.

The Devil
Made Me Do It

At the palace of Ashurbanipal he paused; then shifted
a sidelong glance to a limestone statue hulking in situ:
ragged wings; taloned feet; bulbous, jutting, stubby penis
and a mouth stretched taut in a feral grin. The demon
Pazuzu.

—William Peter Blatty, *The Exorcist*, 1971

The beginning scene in *The Exorcist*, both the book and movie, opens with an archaeological excavation in Iraq. At the site, a priest archaeologist feels a strong southwesterly wind blowing, foreshadowing the arrival of Pazuzu, demon of the southwestern wind and bearer of storms and drought in Assyrian and Babylonian mythology. In the story, however, Pazuzu is the demon that possessed the character Regan. In the beginning, before the existence of man on Earth, Pazuzu was an angel. During Lucifer's revolt against Paradise, Pazuzu became one of his fourteen main lieutenants. At the time of his defeat, he was, like the others, rejected from Paradise. Returning from Hell, he joined the ranks of the gods venerated by the Assyrians and other peoples of ancient Mesopotamia. Pazuzu was revered as a god of winds, storms, and epidemics. According to his moods, he could bring important rain to farmers but also disease. Often, he would intervene with Lamashtu, his barren and jealous wife, to prevent her from stealing babies and causing miscarriage. This, paradoxically, made Pazuzu a protector of pregnant women and their babies. To protect themselves, women invoked Pazuzu with incantations and wore Pazuzu amulets to ward off Lamashtu.

Pazuzu is a Mesopotamian deity dating as far back as the first millennium BCE. He was considered the king of wind demons. A demon of Assyrian origin, he lived in the mountains, sweeping in the southwesterly winds and bringing drought and famine in dry seasons and floods in wet seasons. Pazuzu brings diseases and spreads epidemics (especially malaria) and fevers. As a hybrid being, he is depicted as having a humanoid head with a canine or feline mouth, large teeth, and globular eyes. Pazuzu's body is human with a longer than average torso, similar to that of a dog, but covered with scales like a snake. His hands have claws like a lion. His feet are raptor talons. His tail is a scorpion tail. In his depictions, his penis, ending in a snake's head, is often erect. Pazuzu has two pairs of wings, which is common for the deities of this time. His right hand is raised to heaven and his left hand is lowered to the Earth, meaning life and death, creation and destruction, evoking the eventual image of Baphomet, whose fingers also point in the same manner. This depiction of Pazuzu can be seen on many amulets and figurines found throughout Mesopotamia.

Pazuzu is not the only demonic figure found buried beneath the sands of time. Archaeologists have found more than seventy-five demon-related objects from first millennium BCE in Assyria, Babylon, and Palestine. Many of these objects are amulets or pendants that were placed in houses or worn on the bodies of people to be protected. The most famous of the objects is an Assyrian statuette in bronze of fifteen centimeters high. This statuette is on display at the Louvre Museum. It dates from the eighth century BCE. The demon is represented in his full form with an inscription which declares: "I am Pazuzu, son of Hanpa, the King of the evil spirits of the air who is violently coming out of the mountains raging, it's me!" This statuette is also seen in the film *The Exorcist*, at the time of Regan's exorcism, almost at the end of the film and at the beginning when Father Merrin sees the two dogs fighting. A bronze plaque, also exhibited at the Louvre, shows Pazuzu and Lamashtu in a scene of exorcism. The female demon appears menacing and drives her husband to bring her back to hell. Finally, several exorcism texts were found that explained how to get rid of Pazuzu through exorcism rites.

As an archaeologist, the opening scene in *The Exorcist* and its implication piqued my interest, spurring me to ponder the relationship between the demons of ancient Mesopotamia and modernity. Are the demons of the ancient world still with us today? Then, almost serendipitously, I came across a news story that made me think that perhaps demons, even ancient Mesopotamian demons, may still be dwelling among us, possibly even *possessing* some of us.

On October 5, 2014, the Forsyth County sheriff's deputies searched a suburban home in Clemmons, North Carolina, and discovered the remains of two men who had been missing since 2009. According to autopsy reports, one man was shot once in the back of the head and the other was shot at least seven times, including three times in the head. Who committed these crimes? *Pazuzu.*

The killer's name was Pazuzu Algarad. Before legally changing it, Pazuzu's name was John Lawson. He grew up in the picturesque suburbs of Clemmons. After struggling with what his mother said were mental health issues, he would go on to recruit a brotherhood of disenfranchised people to help him torture, murder, and cannibalize local strangers and bury them in the backyard of his home. According to one psychiatric report, Algarad said he practiced a Sumerian religion that involved a monthly blood sacrifice, usually of a small animal. He said he would have to perform the ritual during what he called the "black moon" in order to appease the Sumerian demons and honor Pazuzu.

Pictures and video taken of the inside of Algarad's house showed a disturbing scene. There were Sumerian markings and occult symbols all over the walls and ceilings of the darkened living room. There were cutout pictures of Sumerian demons and Anunnaki pinned all over the walls. The filthy kitchen where the victims' bodies were prepared for consumption was adorned with more demonic imagery, with strips of fly tape covered in dead flies hanging from above, like hellish party streamers. Leaving the kitchen, you would have to walk through ankle-deep garbage, leading to bedrooms that were piled high with more indistinguishable grime and clutter.

Algarad was arrested and charged with first-degree murder. He and his girlfriend, along with a female friend, were also charged as accessories after the fact to first-degree murder. October 28, at about 3:00 in the morning, guards at Central Prison in Raleigh found Algarad in a pool of blood in his cell. An autopsy report showed he had cut his left arm on the inside of his elbow, as if he were trying to cut off his arm. The report said Algarad had perforated his left brachial artery, likely causing him to bleed to death. He had multiple other deep scratches on his chest, arm, and scalp, along with rib fractures, but the autopsy could not definitively determine how Algarad got the wound that ultimately killed him. Further, the report could not determine if the death was suicide. Algarad had begged the psychiatrists to let him perform his so-called black moon ritual to Pazuzu, fearing that he would anger the demon if he could not appease him. Even his own mother had warned police that if her son were unable to perform his dark moon ritual to Pazuzu, he would likely kill himself.

Could Pazuzu the demon have been behind these murders? Could he have been responsible for the death of his devotee, Algarad? Tonight, as I am writing, there is a very windy front coming in from the southwest. In the dark with only the light from a candle and my computer, I can't help but feel a chill as I notice the wind whistle through the trees. Pazuzu, demon of the southwest wind, is he working in our world today? Certainly, this killer from North Carolina was 100 percent to blame for his heinous acts, but consider who—or what—was his professed inspiration: Pazuzu.

Inspiration, from the Latin *inspirare,* meaning "to breathe or blow into," was originally used to describe when a supernatural being imparts an idea to someone. What is possession but an evil spiritual entity inhabiting a willing person and encouraging them to do evil things in the name of that demon? Although demons may not be tangible, or arguably even real, this recent criminal case leaves me questioning the criteria for demonic possession. Were these criminals simply suffering from psychological disturbances, or had Pazuzu the spirit found willing avatars to carry out his horrendous deeds?

The answers to these questions will be at the heart of this book. Along the way, we will explore the history and lore of sinister relics, asking:

- What is the origin of demons?

- What role did demons play in the development of civilization?

- What is that role today?

- According to the evidence, could demons be real? Can people really become possessed?

- Are curses real? Can material objects contain evil? What about places?

- What can we do to protect ourselves, according to historical records?

It may seem preposterous to ask such questions. Surely, in the age of science, we know better than to believe in silly superstitions about demons and evil entities. Material objects cannot contain evil, right? Consider the alleged case of the prehistoric fertility goddess, commonly referred to as the Goddess of Death, discovered in 1878 in Cyprus. The original owner was Lord Elphont. Within six years of acquiring the statue, all seven of his family members died from mysterious causes. All subsequent owners and their families also died just a few short years after taking the statue into their homes, until the National Museum of Scotland took ownership, after which a museum curator who encountered it also died. Coincidence? Or what about the Florentine Diamond, a 139-carat yellow diamond that is also associated with an extensive line of deaths including that of Queen Elizabeth I, King Farouk of Egypt, Maximilian of Austria, as well as the French King Louis XVI and his notorious wife, Marie Antoinette?

History contains numerous accounts of cursed relics and even places, but as Napoleon Bonaparte famously asked, "What is history, but a fable agreed upon?" Because archaeology is the study of human activity through the recovery and analysis of material culture, many more scientific tools and methods are used to determine the difference between truth and fable. In fact, scientists in Morocco are conducting clinical research into the molecular composition of evil spirits and how they may be more like germs than devils. They even claim to have developed mathematical formulas to prove the existence of evil spirits, as well as calculate their movement and behavior (Dieste, 2014).

Fair warning: This book contains frightening accounts of demonic possession, ancient human sacrifice, and gruesome descriptions of heinous but true archaeological discoveries. This book is not for the faint of heart or easily frightened. If you find that it is too disturbing, try not to worry. The last chapter will include ways to protect yourself and loved ones against malevolent forces, as well as practical advice from experienced exorcists.

"Fear is pain arising from the anticipation of evil."

—Aristotle

CHAPTER 1

It's All in Their Heads

Small, loose stones littered the floor, sparkling like topaz under the flickering orange glow. In the deepest part of the cave, a dark figure rocks back and forth, hands pulling at his hair while unintelligible screams dance off the dense stone walls. A shaman approaches. Others emerge from the darkness until finally, the figure is surrounded: "Gi-lu!" they call out. "Gi-lu!"

The group restrains the figure, flattening him to the floor. Using his knees as calipers, the shaman secures his patient's head. A female places a flint in the shaman's hand. He cuts a small patch of hair from his patient's scalp. Next, the female hands him a reindeer antler with an end whittled to a point. The shaman places the point onto the patient's head. The others begin stomping and erupt with calls to "Gi-lu." With his eyes focused on the bright white patch of scalp, the shaman rubs the antler between his palms, sweat dripping from his prominent brow ridge. The scent of burning hair and bone wafts through the dank enclosure. Is he trying to set the patient's head on fire?

Smattering the floor like garnet embers, blood flickers with each rotation of the antler. After a grueling three hours of careful perforation, a yellow-tinged fluid rushes out of the newly bored hole. The shaman prods the hole with his calloused finger, finally claiming his trophy: a skull disk, which he will wear around his neck. An attendee wipes the patient's head with a piece of animal hide and urinates on the hole. Once cleaned, the shaman packs the hole with reindeer fat and the patient is moved to the furthest part of the cave to heal. The procedure was a success, at least for now. The first forty-eight hours are the most critical.

Having collected some of the patient's blood, the shaman mixes it in rendered fat and ashes, dips his finger into a small shell palette, and begins painting ruddy antlers on the head of a humanoid figure. When finished, he points to the strange chimera grinning back at him from the rippled cave wall and proclaims, "Gi-lu."

Drilling a permanent hole in the skull, or trepanning, is the oldest known surgical procedure, dating back to the late Paleolithic era. Archaeologists have excavated the remains of a Neanderthal man at Mount Zagrou in Iraq, dating back at least 60,000 years. In the second century CE, Greek physician, surgeon, and philosopher Galen described trepanation: "For when we chisel out the fragments of bone we are compelled for safety to put underneath the so-called protectors of the meninx, and if these are pressed too heavily on the brain, the effect is to render the person senseless as well as incapable of all voluntary motion" (Galenos, 1997). A tricky procedure, indeed, but perhaps more bizarre than the antiquity of it is its ubiquity. Trepanning is found in just about every part of the world, from the highest plateaus of China, through the caves of western Europe, to the peaks of the Andes. Why would ancient, let alone prehistoric, people drill holes in one another's heads?

Despite its widespread occurrence, historians and archaeologists disagree about why people performed trepanation. Some believe it was done to cure migraine headaches, convulsions, epilepsy, or traumatic head injury. Others believe it was done to allow the exit or even entrance of evil entities. Pierre Paul Broca, nineteenth-century physician, anthropologist, and namesake of the Broca's area of the brain, theorized that trepanation was done to allow the escape of evil spirits from the head. Other scholars agreed, even publishing that the procedure "may have been considered a sacred operation because the hole would permit the escape of the imprisoned spirit, devil, demon, or other supernatural being" (Wakefield and Dellinger, 1939).

Although disease and injury are known reasons for trepanning, exorcism is also an accepted explanation. The universal popularity of the procedure leads many scholars to believe that trepanning served a ritual function. More recently, archaeological evidence supporting the ritual origin of trepanation was uncovered in a far southern region of Russia, near the Black Sea. Researchers found the skeletal remains of thirty-five humans, distributed among twenty separate graves, dating back to about 5000 and 3000 BCE. One of the graves contained the skeletons of five adults who had all been trepanned. The skulls of two women, three men, and a teenage girl all had holes several centimeters wide. The holes were cut into the same location, the obelion. The obelion is in the back of the head, toward the top. To the archaeologist, this was shocking, as less than 1 percent of all recorded trepanations are located in this part of the head (Arnott, Finger, and Smith, 2014). It is in this area of the brain, above the superior sagittal sinus, where blood collects before flowing into the brain's main venous branches. Thus, opening the skull near the obelion could cause major bleeding and death.

There had been other excavations in this region with similar signs of obelion trepanation, suggesting that these ancient people saw the procedure as being worth the risk. None of the skeletal remains had any signs of illness of trauma, meaning the holes were drilled into their heads when they were healthy. To researchers, this was a clear sign that trepanation had been done as a ritual, rather than a medical procedure. This was confirmation of Broca's original theory. He was intrigued to find that people all over the world performed trepanation, but amazed when discovering how well it had been done in some specific regions, like Peru. Broca originally believed that trepanation was performed as a type of surgical exorcism.

Of all the prehistoric trepanned skulls found to date, the largest number of samples come from Peru, where they were drilling holes in their heads since at least 400 BCE. Upon learning this, Broca determined that trepanation proved the ancient people of the pre-conquest New World were far more advanced than other scholars initially thought. However, trepanning was not the only cranial procedure performed in the ancient world. Artificial cranial deformation or modification, which resulted in elongated skulls, is also found in Mesoamerican populations. Although some claim that these elongated skulls have some sort of extraterrestrial connection, the real reason for the practice of skull binding is a bit more obscure, hence, the misinformation. The motivation behind skull elongation is indeed otherworldly but has less to do with aliens, and more to do with demons.

Elongated Skulls

The Mesoamericans saw the head a sort of spiritual receptacle. Their unique concept of the soul was called *tonalli*, the root of which, *tona*, points to an association with the sun. The *tonalli* was a soul that derived its energy and power from the sun's heat. This powerful spiritual heat resided in the head. This belief was shared by the Nahuatl people of Mesoamerica. When the children of the Nahuatl were born, they believed the gods breathed the *tonalli* into them. This process awakened the infant's consciousness and united him with his destiny.

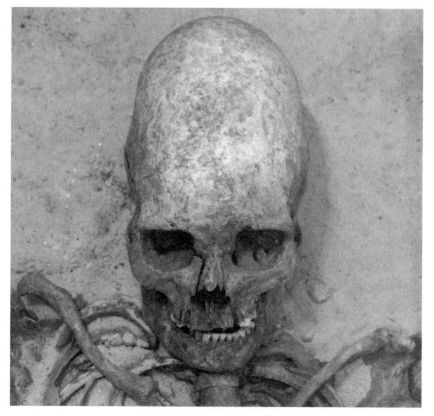

Elongated skull in situ.

There is one problem, though. Infants have a soft skull with an open fontanel, the membranous gap between the cranial bones that allows the skull to stretch in response to the natural expansion of the brain during development. This gap in the skull made newborns especially vulnerable. The risk was twofold. The infant could lose his *tonalli* from that opening, or perhaps worse, evil spirits could enter the infant's head. To prevent the loss of the infant's soul and/or demonic possession, his head was tightly bound. This binding gradually forced the skull to form into a conical shape. The Mesoamericans were not the only people who connected the head to the spirit world. Evidence in the archaeological record indicates that the head has often been an object of special spiritual significance.

Skull Cults

In addition to drilling and binding the head, ancient people performed other types of surgical exorcisms. In Italy, Germany, France, Yugoslavia, and China, skulls have been found that were broken apart at the base in order to extract the brain. Archaeologists argue that apart from ritual cannibalism and headhunting, the skulls may have been emptied to rid them of evil entities. Veneration of the human head was common in the ancient world, but evidence of just how sophisticated it was can be found in some of the oldest sites.

In the Neolithic communities in the territory of modern Turkey and the Levant, skull cults were quite common. Evidence found at Göbekli Tepe, at a site at least 11,000 years old, that it was once used by skull cults. Monuments at the site formed oval walls, and in the center of each were two T-shaped megaliths, the largest measuring more than five meters in height. Analysis suggests that Göbekli Tepe was used as a temple, but not all scholars agree. This site has both surprised and puzzled archaeologists because the hunter-gatherers who inhabited the region hadn't yet learned agriculture, so how were they able to erect such monumental limestone structures?

One theory about the site is that it functioned as a temple. Recent excavations seem to support this theory. Archaeologists have unearthed about seven hundred fragments of human bones, of which more than four hundred are parts of skulls. Why did these scraps attract scientists' attention? These skulls had evidence of trepanation, many strange incisions, and also ocher marks. There were no signs of healing, indicating that the skull modifications were made shortly after death.

Researchers have been unable to determine to whom these skulls belonged. Where they revered ancestors or killed enemies? It is also not clear whether the ritual was conducted here, or if the skulls were brought to Göbekli Tepe from somewhere else. One thing is for sure: Inhabitants of Göbekli Tepe had a special relationship to the heads of the deceased. More examples point to this, like the headless figure with a phallus on one of the T-shaped monoliths, statues with separated heads, as well as predatory animals clutching in their claws something resembling a severed head. There is also a limestone figure of a creature on its knees holding a human head in its hands.

Clearly, the skull was a sacred object that needed to be protected after death, as well as in life. The Dayak people of Borneo, for example, believed that after death, one's body was vulnerable to evil spirits and therefore must be exorcised to protect the deceased and their family from demons. A great feast lasted for nearly a month and included rituals performed to relieve the deceased's family from their demonic possession. For the family members to be considered rid of the demons, they were required to undergo a merciless purification ritual. First, the surviving family selected a human victim. Then, the victim was chained to a sacrificial post while the surviving male relatives of the deceased took turns dancing and torturing the victim. They abused the victim with spears to induce the greatest pain possible because the grislier the torture, the happier the souls of the departed were supposed to be as they made their way to heaven. When the victim was brutalized beyond the point of survival, he fell to the ground like a human piñata and was decapitated. A priestess collected the victim's blood and sprinkled it onto the family members. Then, the decapitated head was either added to the bones of the deceased or attached to the top of a post (Hertz, 2008). Could a ritual like this have occurred at Göbekli Tepe? Some archaeologists believe it is possible, but we may never know for sure.

Nevertheless, the widespread belief that somehow the human head could be infiltrated by spirits, whether good or evil, begs the question: Why? Why the head? It would seem obvious to contemporary people because we know about the importance of the brain. However, understanding the role of the brain to consciousness is a relatively new development. In the fourth century BCE, Aristotle proposed that the brain was a nonprimary organ that merely served as a cooling agent for the heart and functioned like a radiator. He explained that the heart, being the origin of fiery emotions like love and hate, was warm. Therefore, blood would go from the warm heart to the brain to be cooled. To Aristotle, this meant that the heart was the source of consciousness. His reasoning was that because the heart is warm, active, and filled with blood, it is logically the seat of the soul. Aristotle's anatomic findings dominated medical thinking for the next five hundred years. Eventually, the Roman physician Galen would realize that cognition occurred in the brain, rather than the heart, as Aristotle had suggested. He reached his conclusion after observing the effects of brain injuries on the mental abilities of his patients. Galen concluded that the brain was the seat of consciousness.

If the idea that consciousness resides in the brain is supposedly new, then how did ancient people understand the role the brain played in cognition? Did they simply observe the before and after of traumatic brain injury, something that would have been frequent in a harsh and primitive world? Or was this not a question of physiology as much as it was spirituality? Like the Mesoamericans, other nature-dwelling people may have thought that because the head is closest to the sky, it is better positioned to receive and transmit spiritual energy. In a religious sense, there are many faiths that encourage a head covering, recognizing the head as a sort of satellite receiver that can be tuned in to spiritual messages from above. Would this thinking apply to evil spirits? Thinking of evil as residing above us, rather than below, is only strange when imagining it from a contemporary perspective, one that has been enculturated to recognize hellish tropes like horned red devils that poke burning sinners with pitchforks in a fiery underworld. Where did this idea originate?

When Evil Came Down to Earth

In many contemporary cultures, demons are not located above our heads but rather below our feet. We do not typically imagine demons coming down from the heavens because Hell is an underworld. However, the belief that the spirit world is somewhere in the skies above is shared by a surprising number of ancient people. Man has celestialized his gods in such a way as to connect them with the sun, moon, planets, and stars. Even Lucifer, a name synonymous with modern concepts of "the Devil," began his story in the sky.

Ezekiel describes how God created Lucifer to be a perfected being: "Thou wast perfect in thy ways from the day that thou wast created, till iniquity was found in thee" (Ezekiel 28:15 KJV).

This verse points to a history of Lucifer as an ascended figure, one that began as perfect and holy but fell out of favor with God. The name Lucifer became synonymous with a name of the Devil in Christianity, partially due to the seventeenth-century epic poem *Paradise Lost* by John Milton. In his poem, Milton presents Lucifer, whom he calls "Satan," as a proud, ambitious angel who falls from grace after rebelling against God. In this account, the fallen angel enters the Garden of Eden and takes the shape of a snake to tempt Eve to eat from the tree of knowledge. Literally translated from Latin, the name Lucifer means "bearer of light," which was in reference to the planet Venus. Venus was also called the "morning star" because it is very bright in the sky and can be observed with the naked eye in the morning before sunrise.

Three planets, Venus, Mars, and Jupiter, can all be seen in daylight. When a personification of the Morning Star is encountered in myths, however, it is generally accepted to mean Venus or Mars. What was it about the Morning Star that captured the imagination of the ancients, and why was it so often linked to evil? This interpretation was not exclusive to the astronomers of the East, nor to the mythmakers of the West. The Morning Star demanded reverence and, at times, even human sacrifices from a place you may least expect—the Great Plains of North America.

The Sacrifice to the Morning Star

Scholars believe that, of the Great Plains peoples, the Pawnees had the most highly developed cosmology. Their primary god was named Tirawa. He was the purely spiritual creator of the universe, ruling over a variety of lesser gods who were divided into two groups, the gods of Earth and the gods of Heaven. The gods of Heaven were, as you might expect, superior to the gods of Earth. These heavenly spirits were associated with animals and helped elite people in Native American secret societies. By contrast, the gods of Earth were associated with stars responsible for helping average people. The most important of these gods were the Morning and Evening Stars, representing the male and female. The origin of man was linked to the union of these two stars, oddly similar to the Rosicrucian alchemical marriage philosophy of seventeenth-century Europe.

Just as Lucifer came down to tempt man with eating of the forbidden tree, gifting him with the knowledge of good and evil, and just like the story of Prometheus defying the gods to descend to Earth to give men fire, the Pawnee believe their Morning Star god also came down to Earth to give man secret wisdom. Members of the secret societies of the Skidi band of Pawnee closely guarded these ancient secrets, and a ritual was devised to show gratitude to the Morning Star for giving man these gifts. This ritual, known simply as the Morning Star Ceremony, was a reenactment of the Morning Star descending to Earth to give man wisdom.

In the late spring or summer of years when Mars would be the visible morning star, the Morning Star would appear to a warrior in a dream. The warrior would be unable to sleep or rest, becoming consumed with the idea of finding a human sacrifice to appease the Morning Star. He and a band of men would venture to the land of their enemy, all the while hunting and making offerings to the Morning Star to reassure him that the time for human sacrifice was soon to come. When they found their victim, a young girl, they would send a message back to the village so that preparations for the ceremony could begin. The warrior called the girl *Opirikuts,* or "mighty star of fire," and warned the others not to touch her, for if they did, their lives would be in danger. She must remain pure to be a suitable sacrifice to the Morning Star.

Back at the village, the priests would clear a circle and dig a fireplace to use as a lodge. When the warrior returned, a fire was lit, and the smoke offered to the gods. Songs symbolizing the union of the Morning and Evening Star were sung, and a mystery play acted out until the warrior faced east, speaking directly to the Morning Star. The warrior would call upon this entity with the following invocation: "I am praying to you as you directed, and we are seeking a sacrifice as you wished. I ask you to show yourself!" (Linton, 1926).

After the invocation, the star would shine brighter, as if in response. Celebrations continued through the night until it was time for the Morning Star to rise, at which point the leader would give a final invocation before putting on war paint. After an evening of somewhat Luciferian invocations, the leader would become possessed by the Morning Star. Four priests representing the four cardinal directions officiated the ceremony and helped to build large scaffolding on which to hang the girl. Once the Morning Star rose higher in the sky, the other warriors howled like wolves. The sacrifice had begun.

The girl was brought to the fire, undressed and purified in the smoke. Then, the right side of her body was painted red, the sacred color of the Morning Star. The left side of her body was painted black to symbolize night. Dressed in a black robe and shoes, she was given a headdress of twelve black-tipped eagle feathers, arranged like a fan.

In a procession of chanting priests, she was led to the scaffold and suspended by the wrists. Before the sacrifice, men wearing owl skins around their necks took their position on each side of the girl, symbolizing that they were conduits of wisdom and messengers of the Morning Star. Finally, the girl's body was cut open and her organs caught by a guardian. This guardian violently pushed his hand into the girl's thoracic cavity and painted his face with her blood. The girl's liver was cut into pieces and eaten. After the initial dissection of the body, the girl's dangling body was shot at with as many arrows as possible so her lifeless, reddened corpse resembled the rays of light emanating from the Morning Star. The last Morning Star Ceremony took place in 1838.

Although rare, human sacrifices in North America occurred in some tribes. In South America, however, human sacrifice was a sophisticated system claiming the lives of many innocent victims. Interestingly, historians have identified similarities between Skidi Pawnee and Aztec sacrificial ceremonies. Aztec manuscripts depict the same Skidi Pawnee–style scene of a victim hanging from scaffolding, shot to death with arrows to become the personification of a deity. Likewise, in both Skidi Pawnee and Aztec rituals, the victims' bodies were cut open and their hearts ripped out. Human sacrifice, a brutally corporal method to honor celestial gods, will be examined more closely in chapter 4.

What would make ancient and primitive people believe in unseen spirits in the first place? Most people would say it is because humans try to rationalize the world around them, attempting to understand it by making up stories to communicate abstract ideas and cope with the things they fear due to a lack of understanding. Essentially, it is all in their heads. If evil is a construct of human developmental understanding, then evil entities are the personification of these understandings. Are demons then merely products of the human imagination? According to American psychologist Julian Jaynes (1920–1997), all spirits came from the literal heads of early man.

Cognitive Archaeology

It may seem out of place to discuss psychology or philosophy in a book about archaeology. However, popular culture's understanding of archaeology is not always correct. The discipline is far more than digging in the dirt. There are seven key stages in archaeology. The stage most often depicted in movies and television is the full excavation, but archaeology is so much more than that one snapshot in time. It is in the analysis of discoveries where we find truth. Part of that analysis is indeed scientific. This part is referred to as archaeometry and includes the application of scientific techniques to analyze artifacts, such as radiocarbon dating, scanning electron microscopy, X-rays, and so on. Scientific techniques can tell us a lot about artifacts, but it cannot tell us everything. Thus, an archaeologist and/or historian must use other methods, referred to as qualitative methods. Qualitative methods look more closely at "the meanings, concepts definitions, characteristics, metaphors, symbols, and description of things" (Berg and Lune, 2014). This is something to keep in mind moving forward. While this book presents various artifacts and sites, I frequently use a theoretical perspective referred to as "cognitive archaeology" to examine the ideas presented. Cognitive archaeology deals with concepts and perception, particularly in the areas of religion, belief, symbolism, iconography, and consciousness. This cross-disciplinary approach to scholarship, increasingly rare today, is exactly what made Jaynes so much of a trailblazer.

While working as a psychology professor at Princeton University, Julian Jaynes published a very controversial theory about the emergence of the human mind. He believed that until just a few thousand years ago, people had no introspection and no concept of "self." In short, they had no subjective consciousness. Jaynes calls this the bicameral mind (Jaynes, 2003). The brain is divided into a god side and a human side. The human side heard voices and experienced them as coming from the gods. These gods were not judgmental, ethical, or unknowable gods, but rather personal guides, a kind of personal problem-solver for every human being. They answered the problems for which no routine response existed.

To Jaynes, consciousness is a process, not an immediate sensation or state of being. It is a way of thinking that enables people to make considerations and decisions for themselves. How did the world look before consciousness existed? Jaynes uses the Greek epic *The Iliad,* from the eighth century BCE, to illustrate his point. He claims that this story was written in a period in which the bicameral mentality was already in decline, but still "operational." In *The Iliad,* humans hear the voices of gods in times of stress, similarly to the way schizophrenics may sometimes hear voices telling them what to do. Jaynes argues this is the bicameral mind that has not yet unified and does not make conscious decisions. In a sense, this person makes no decisions at all; he only acts in the way the god side of his mind tells him to.

Jaynes speculates about the origin of the split nature of the bicameral mind. He asks us to imagine a phase in the evolution of the human species in which there was a primitive language that was used only for basic communication. There was no inner dialogue yet. When humans started "hearing" their own inner dialogue, they obeyed it because the inner voice may have simply been an audible memory echoing the voice of a clan leader. As this stage advances, the voices may have become increasingly intelligent and unfamiliar because they were creations of the person's own unique thoughts rather than memories of what others said. As a result, they may have been attributed to a higher being.

Between about 1250 and 1000 BCE, there was a catastrophically disruptive event that became known as the Bronze Age collapse. Within this time, both cultures and governments collapsed. There were changes in climate that resulted in mass migration, wars, and violence. The social order was pushed to the brink, and we begin to see the first evidence for the crumbling of the bicameral mind emerge in the historical and archaeological record. Texts show the internal struggle of humankind and kings who fret because they cannot help their people. The gods no longer instruct them on what to do. They bow before an empty throne in grief. The gods have left humankind behind to think for themselves and to make decisions using their own internal powers of reasoning. In "The Poem of the Righteous Sufferer," found on a cuneiform tablet from the time of King Marduk of Babylon around 1230 BCE, there are multiple references to gods who have left man:

> *My god has forsaken me and disappeared,*
>
> *My goddess has failed me and keeps at a distance.*
>
> *The benevolent angel who walked beside me has departed,*
>
> *My companion has become a wretch and a devil . . . .*
>
> *I called to my god, but he did not show his face,*
>
> *I prayed to my goddess, but she did not raise her head.*
> (Annus and Lenzi, 2010)

When the bicameral mind encountered this stress, or breakdown, as Jaynes refers to it, humankind had to make decisions that had further-reaching implications. Since they no longer had the voices of their gods in their heads, they started devising ways to contact them. This included studying astrology, omens, casting stones, reading the intestines of animals, and so on. These all became methods that could relay the will of the gods that still existed but were no longer heard. Using these methods projected the will of the gods into the outside world. Decision-making was therefore still an external process at this stage. What emerged from this stage of psychological development were priests, prophets, and oracles. Over the next six centuries, visions or auditory hallucinations of the gods were only experienced by these individuals. Drugs were also needed in order to "hear" gods. When considering this explanation, it brings to mind the Egyptian word *ka,* the meaning of which scholars continue to disagree on. Some interpret it to mean "voice," while others describe it as something akin to a soul of a human or god that survived the death of the physical body and could enter possess an image or statue. Could Jaynes's theory explain why the ancients started making and carrying idols?

The time between 1000 and 500 BCE is notable. This is a period sometimes referred to as the Axial Age. German philosopher Karl Jaspers coined the term to describe this time because he thought this period was the axis of world history. From the earliest times of civilization to around 1000 BCE, human cultures everywhere progressed rather slowly. However, in a matter of a few hundred years from approximately 1000 BCE, something unexplained happened and cultures exploded. With this explosion came complex ideas like religion, philosophy, government, and even science, the underpinnings of which still influence our modern social structure and belief systems.

What started as internalized ideas ended up becoming externalized structures. Did demons and spiritual entities begin in ancient man's head as an idea, then manifest into the material world as a feature of a newly structured belief system until finally materializing as idols so that man could cope with the psychological stress of the breakdown of his own mind? Perhaps this explains the appearance of so many statues, amulets, and figurines of gods and demons in the archaeological record of man's most ancient civilizations.

To prehistoric man, it may seem that the origin of demons was quite literally in their heads. When man began settling into more complex social groups, the stresses he encountered resulted in what Jaynes believed to be a mental breakdown that led to a realization that the gods who once walked beside him were now gone. Their divine voices were now silenced in his mind, only to be heard again with the help of shamanistic ritual and psychedelic drugs. The archaeological record is rich with artifacts depicting deities, including demons. Did the ancients try to bring the gods (and demons) back, by making and carrying idols in the form of statues, amulets, and figurines?

By at least the fourth millennium BCE, the first urban centers formed in the land known as the cradle of civilization. These early civilizations began with the Sumerian people and would later include the Akkadians, Babylonians, and Assyrians. In Mesopotamia, the area between the Tigris and Euphrates Rivers, in what is now Iraq, there was an instantaneous boom of cultural development. Scholars describe the Sumerians as exhibiting an unusually creative intellect. In a mere three hundred years—a historical blink of an eye—huge complex structures, theology, technologies, and governments emerged. Inventions unlike anything the world had ever known began to manifest and would forever change the course of human culture.

Such high levels of civilization were responsible for creating a more unified culture in the region that appears profoundly marked by the belief in all kinds of evil demons and protective entities. The line between evil demons and protective demons is often unclear because the Sumerians would enlist the help of one demon to fight against another demon. Throughout

Mesopotamian history, the belief in the existence of evil or protective forces appears strongly anchored in culture. The threats of disease or death hovered over people with often precarious living conditions, and perhaps led to the appointment of some of the first professional exorcists trained to battle these evil forces. The methods these ancient exorcists used in their rituals more than four thousand years ago are shockingly similar to those employed in the modern Catholic Church.

• CHAPTER 2 •

The Cradle of Evil

For weeks, the young farmhand had suffered from increasingly severe headaches that radiated from his temples to his neck. At night, he would lie in bed, burning with a fever, leaving him to long for the southwesterly breeze to sweep through his room and relive his suffering. When he was not suffering from the heat, he was shivering in the cold, waking up every few hours, only to find that he had again wet the bed. These restless nights left him exhausted, with bloodshot eyes, ringing in the ears, nausea, vomiting, and vertigo. His father took notice and urged him to seek help. After trying various treatments, none of which were successful, his condition worsened. His symptoms became unbearable, and he drifted into an almost catatonic state, seemingly detached from reality.

Until one evening, delirious, he found himself lying in bed with his father standing over him praying. As his outstretched body convulsed, a priest stood at his bedside, demanding to know the name of the demon who had caused this. For three days, the demon refused to divulge his identity. The priest, unrelenting, called out to the demon, "Whether you be a strange spirit, whose name nobody knows, or a roving spirit, or a roaming spirit, or the tortured spirit of someone who was abandoned, abused, lonely, drowned, starved, burned, murdered, or an evil spirit sent from hell, give me your name!" The priest anointed the young man's head with oil and water that had been blessed. He then flushed the young man's ear using a solution of beer and medicinal herbs until out streamed fluid and black bits of dead flies.

Upon realizing what his body just purged, he cried out, "I am truly grieved, confused and troubled. Shall I kneel for your judgment? Save me so that I may not be wronged!" The priest comforted the crying young man. He instructed the father to administer the ear solution along with other medications and advised that his son would be fully cured within a month. He left the grateful family to pray for thanks and celebrate in their victory over the Lord of Flies.

This account was based on a series of Sumerian exorcism texts that are over 3,600 years old. Similar methods and dialogue between the priests and possessed were outlined in these ancient clay tablets. These were considered medical texts, in addition to spiritual ones, so their methods and practices blurred the lines between body and spirit. The ancient Sumerian exorcism tablets were discovered by archaeologists in the Royal Library of Ashurbanipal. The Library of Ashurbanipal, named after the last great king of the Neo-Assyrian Empire, contained thousands of clay tablets dating as far back as the seventh century BCE. The original tablets are in the British Museum. The museum has about 1,000 cuneiform tablets, of which 660 reference exorcism.

One exorcism rite is illustrated on a bronze figure of the demon Pazuzu, whose outstretched arms hold a tablet depicting symbols similar to those on the boundary stones, a type of stone document that records the end of one land and the beginning of another. It is a small amulet, only about five-and-a-half inches high by three-and-a-half inches wide. It is referred to as the Hell Plaque.

The Mesopotamian Hell Plaque

On the top first row are divine symbols like those typically found on boundary stones, including the symbol of Utu. Utu (later known as Shamash) was the ancient Mesopotamian sun god. He represented truth, justice, and morality. According to Sumerian mythology, Utu was the twin brother of the goddess Inanna, the Queen of Heaven. He would spend his days traveling through the sky in a sun chariot, keeping a watchful eye on all the humans below. It was believed that he was very powerful and would intervene between demons and humans to help those in distress and enforce divine retribution. Utu was depicted as a solar disc. This appeared as a circle with a four-pointed star pointing to the cardinal directions, like a compass. Overlapping that were four wavy lines stemming from the center between each of the points on the four-pointed star. This symbol is seen all over Mesopotamian art, as it symbolized warmth and light from the sun, as well as power. Also included on the top, are the symbols for other deities such as Ea, depicted by a mace with ram's head, Marduk by a spearhead, Adad by a lightning fork, Nebo by his double staff, Ishtar by an eight-pointed star, Sin by the crescent, and the Sibitti, identified with the Pleiadian star system and depicted as seven circles.

The second row shows seven *gallu* (the earliest root of the word "ghoul"), demons that carried victims off to the Mesopotamian underworld, having the heads of animals. These animal-human hybrid beings are a common element among human depictions of demons. It is a theme that arises from the pressures of adapting from a primitive or wild existence to one that is more civilized. This theme is found throughout ancient art and protoliterature, hinting to a dualistic concept of "good versus evil," or the struggle between wild man and civilized man. This binary struggle will be more closely examined in the next chapter.

The third row of the exorcism tablet shows that actual exorcism rite. In the middle, a possessed person lies on a bed. At the head and foot of the bed are priests, identified by their fishlike robes, which indicate that they are priests of the water god, Ea. A demon behind the right priest holds two other demons at bay. The other priest holds a lamp, which symbolizes the god of fire, Nusku.

The last row shows objects such as a bowl, water bladder, two jars, and various foods. These are offerings for the demons. In the very center of this last row, a large depiction of the demon Lamashtu holds a snake each hand. She breastfeeds two pigs and kneels on a donkey, which is her symbol. The donkey is resting on a ship, sailing on water where there are fish swimming from left to right. To Lamashtu's left is her threatening husband, Pazuzu, who is trying to attack her with a whip. Pazuzu was summoned by the priests to defend the patient from her. This is a common theme in the Pazuzu/Lamashtu story. Pazuzu was often invoked to protect pregnant women and mothers against Lamashtu, because she would steal their babies out of jealousy. This was the explanation for miscarriages, stillborn infants, and sudden infant death, making tablets and amulets of Pazuzu some of the most popular in the first millennium in Mesopotamia.

Known as the Hell Plaque, this amulet held by the demon Pazuzu would be placed at the bedside of the possessed. It depicts the demon Lamashtu, Pazuzu's wife, on the front of the plate.

In the temple-schools of Mesopotamia, students learned exorcism rituals, how to mix healing ointments, perform astrology, and treat diseases as possessions. These skills seem archaic now, but the temple-schools served as the first medical schools. They even trained their students on the study of contract law, ethics, medical billing, and accounting. They were hubs of intellectual activity. The temple priests produced textbooks to train young medical students, the candidates of the priesthood. As a result of the Sumerians' meticulous record-keeping, archaeologists are able to study their early medical knowledge and religious beliefs.

What they have found is that the Sumerians believed certain spirits caused specific diseases, which could be identified through a patient's symptoms. This spirit entity would enter the body through the patient's head. It was important for the priest to know the name of the entity so that he could prescribe the right treatment. It was as though the names of the demons were the names of the diseases. For instance, one tablet refers to the practice of rubbing someone's head with butter and milk so they would be cleansed of the "head disease of heaven" (Thompson, 1924). Possessions in Mesopotamia were not limited to head diseases. Symptoms of demonic possession could be felt throughout the entire body. According to another tablet, symptoms of demonic possession can begin in the muscles of the body. The possessed patient can have fever and chills, intestinal problems, pain in the abdomen that radiates to the back, as well as chest pain (ibid.). In this case, the demon did not attack the head, however, the treatment calls for purifying the patient with water, then wrapping his head with a bandage and juniper leaves. He must leave this bandage on for one full day, then discard it. This method supposedly drew the demon out of the patient's head.

One method, as humorous as it is interesting, is the act of modeling clay figures of demons in order to have them battle. Far from pitting a titan against a titan, this was more like a primitive game of Rock'em Sock'em Robots. The priest would instruct the patient to make a figurine of the demon, and then the patient would raise his hand and say, "That unknown ghost, I have made a figurine of him" (Scurlock, 2006). Then, the priest would purify a clay pit, put atta (wheat flour) into it, and the next morning would say, "I will buy clay from the potter's pit for a representation of whatever is evil. You, pinch off clay and make figurines of the male and female witch" (ibid.). The patient would then present those figures and pray that the demon takes the clay figure as a substitute, that his spirit may leave his body. The ancient texts actually describe how to make these clay scapegoat figures. You were to mix clay from a potter's pit with tallow and wax. Then you would say three times to the evil spirits this figure is "like myself; his flesh is like the appearance of my flesh. I have mixed clay from the pure mountains, tallow, and wax. I have made a representation of him" (Thompson, 1924). Then, you would pose the figure and even feed it, saying, "Eat this! You are my substitute. Drink! You have been provisioned, a dowry has been given to you. Little dwarf, you have been completely fitted out. As my substitute" (Scurlock, 2006). When the spirit entered the clay figure, a separate clay figure of an adversarial demon would be placed with it so that they could do battle.

Another method of purification was to make a funerary offering to the spirit, such as bread, beer, or water. The patient would take the skull of a dog and fill it with beer, then pour the beer onto the ground and dedicate it to the demon. In this method, the demon would be drawn to the foods and thus lured out of the patient. Although clearly strange, there was an element of reasoning behind it. The Sumerians did not believe in just one type of spirit. They believed in entities similar to demons, devils, and even ghosts, all of which could enter a person through possession. Some were demons from the underworld and others were simply sad, lost souls. In order to know the difference, the exorcist would pay close attention to the patient's symptoms, as well as consult his manual. For example, if a person in life was unloved, abused, and neglected to the point wherein they were starved to death, that tortured soul would seek to inhabit the body of someone else. Once in that body, however, their tortured nature would be expressed in the patient. This could make the patient feel symptoms of depression, loneliness, nausea, loss of appetite, chill, and weakness. Therefore, the healing rite, or exorcism, could include making a nice meal for the spirit and offering it positive affirmations, in addition to medicinal herbs.

This practice offers a glimpse into the minds and hearts of ancient people. Regardless of the science or logic, it does indeed show a level of compassion on their part. Rather than demonize even a demon, they sought to understand and make an emotional appeal. This is in contrast to the modern depictions of exorcism and possession, which usually portray coarse, demanding exorcists who show no mercy. To the Sumerians, things were not always black and white. This accounts for the popularity of Pazuzu as a protective figure, while also being the harbinger of evil. They believed that even the most harmful demon could be helpful.

Everyday Demons

The belief in a wide variety of evil demons and protective spirits heavily influenced the life of Mesopotamians. The label of demons as avatars of evil allowed ancient people to identify a threat like disease or bad weather so that they might fight it by using the proper rituals. Throughout Mesopotamian history, the belief in the existence of evil and protective forces was rooted deep into their psyche. They did not see these entities the same way we might today. Although they were evil, they also defended against evil. The lines between good and bad were sometimes blurred, or perhaps more accurately, seen as harmful and useful. The threats of disease and death that hovered over people, whose precarious living conditions made them more vulnerable to disease and misfortune, made it necessary to appoint others who were well-versed in understanding how to fight against these threats. Henceforth, the exorcist priest would become a legitimized profession, making it an important part of civil society. These holy leaders and protophysicians made it possible to circumscribe the dangers of everyday life and implement ways to prevent or even defeat them.

Around the third millennium, priests started creating a vast repertoire of demons with superhuman powers and invented all kinds of rituals and magical treatments in order to provide a cure. To fight against the demonic possession that they believed responsible for serious physical and spiritual disease, conjuring rituals were established to summon protective demons, like Pazuzu. Archaeologists have excavated a host of protective demons in houses and administrative centers. Often, these clay figures were buried under their foundations as a defense against potential threats.

Many Mesopotamian demons originated as monsters, like Anzu, an enormous bird with a lion's head. Anzu is depicted as so big that he caused tornadoes and storms just by flapping his wings. Anzu stole the Tablet of Destinies, on which the highest god wrote the destiny of all the world. Anzu was finally murdered by the god Ninurta, who returned the tablet to the rightful owner. Some Mesopotamian monsters are man-beast hybrid creatures. One of these animal-human hybrid demons was Kusarikku, or "Bull-Man." Kusarikku is a demon with the body of a man above the waist and a bull below the waist. He also has the horns and ears of a bull. As a protector demon, Kusarikku actually helps people fight evil and chaos.

Other Mesopotamian demons seemed rather innocuous and were connected to elements of nature and related to fertility of both people and plants. Mesopotamian demons play a central role in the creation of man. The vicious and destructive goddess Tiamat decided to destroy all other gods, so she created a large army of demons. The other gods decided that Tiamat must be destroyed, but they were all too afraid of her to try. Marduk, god of the city of Babylon, agreed to kill Tiamat in exchange for being made the supreme god. Marduk was also called Bel, meaning "Lord." The etymology of Marduk's name can be seen in other demonic names like Ba'al, the child-eating god of the Canaanites; Beelzebub, associated with Satan in the Christian tradition; and even in the name Jezebel. Marduk kills Tiamat to make Heaven and Earth, and cuts her body through the middle. The rivers Tigris and Euphrates flow from her eyes.

An important point about demons in this period in human history is that only the gods could control the demons. They could command demons to either hurt or help people, positioning them as the mediators between gods and men. This made them central to maintaining the fragile balance of the ancient world. The people of Mesopotamia embraced their beliefs in demons and spread them to other cultures over time, and even shaped the Christian view of demons. This is due in large part to the Babylonian captivity of Jews in ancient history.

Babylonian Exile

The kingdom of Judah came under Babylonian rule at the end of the seventh century BCE, after the Babylonians overthrew the Assyrian Empire. Judah had been a vassal state of the Assyrian Empire since the mid-eighth century BCE. In the confusion that arose after the fall of the Assyrian Empire, the Egyptians tried to seize power in the western lands. King Jehoiakim of Judah joined the Egyptians but was defeated by the Babylonians. After the fall of the Jewish capital Jerusalem in 597 BCE, the Babylonian king Nebuchadnezzar II deported the new king Jehoiachin, his court, and most of the Jewish elite to Babylon. Two later Jewish uprisings led to further deportations in 586 BCE, when the Babylonians also destroyed the Temple of Solomon and most of Jerusalem, and 582 BCE.

Although not treated very well, the Jews in Babylon were left alone to marry, raise a family, farm, buy property, and raise capital. Despite the absence of bloody persecutions, the exile was traumatic for the Jews. They felt imprisoned and mistreated. While they were subject to foreign domination, their land, which had been assigned to them by their God, was destroyed. Exile therefore had an immense influence on the Jewish identity. The Jews would become closer as a people and as a religious group, but they would also come to adopt new ideas and customs.

When the Persian king Cyrus the Great conquered Babylon, he ended the Babylonian Exile in 538 BCE. Cyrus allowed the Jews to return to Judah, after which they rebuilt Jerusalem in the period between 520 and 515 BCE. The new temple was inaugurated in 516 BCE. When the Jews returned, they were different. The time they spent in Babylon had influenced their culture, particularly affecting the young.

The Jews brought with them all sorts of Babylonian customs and beliefs. They had taken over a lot of the language and practices; many did not even know their own writing anymore, only the Aramaic script used in Babylon. The Jews created the Babylonian Talmud, which contains many ideas borrowed from Babylonian mythology. The Talmud, literally "the teaching," is the fundamental work of the Jewish religion. The Talmud takes verbal explanations, questions and answers, issues such as riddles and gives them binding form. The Talmud contains two works: the Mishnah of Palestine, the canonical collection of Jewish laws, and the Gemara, the discussions of these laws, which were recorded in Babylon. Part of the mythology they brought with them included demonology. Many of the demons of Babylon are shared with the Jewish faith. A good example of this cultural influence is the Talmudic privy demon known as Shed Bet ha-Kise. It is a new iteration of the well-known Akkadian demon, Šulak.

Here is an important reminder to bear in mind that when reading or discussing Mesopotamian history. Mesopotamia is a geographical region, whereas the Sumerians, Akkadians, Babylonians, and Assyrians were all nations or empires that ruled in Mesopotamia at times overlapping a period of nearly three thousand years. Generally speaking, the Sumerians came first, then the Akkadians, then the Babylonians, and then the Assyrians. Now, do not let this very condensed history lull you into thinking it was this clean and linear. Including a complete history of the culture in this region would take far more than just this book, let alone this chapter. The general timeline is meant only to get an idea of the cultural expansion, and to explain the similarities. Although each group of people was unique, they all shared many cultural characteristics, including language to a certain extent, which is how scholars have been able to interpret Sumerian. Thus, scholars are also able to recognize the paths through which cultural information spread, as in the case of the Babylonian Talmud. The experience of exile led to a cultural infusion for the Jewish people, whether they were initially open to it or not. The mythologies they kept have even found their way into Christian culture, as Christianity came from Judaism. The toilet demon is an example of one such enduring, possibly strange, myth.

The Mesopotamian Toilet Demon

Many passages in the Babylonian Talmud warn against "Shed Bet ha-Kise," the "toilet demon." There were a variety of warnings about toilet behavior and one's safety and defense against this toilet demon. One warning was that after coming from the toilet, one mustn't have sexual intercourse immediately or else his children will be epileptic (Bamberger, 2013). Again, we see that epilepsy is associated with demonic entities. The notion that epilepsy is caused by demons was widely believed in ancient Mesopotamia. The Babylonian Talmud prescribed the wearing of certain amulets to prevent epilepsy attacks. This is parallel to the beliefs of the Akkadians, who warned of the same demon whom they called Šulak, who caused similar symptoms. The demon from both the Akkadian records and Babylonian Talmud resembles a lion or sometimes a goat being, lives in toilets, and causes epilepsy, strokes, or sudden falls. The Akkadian version of the toilet demon is mentioned in a medical handbook used in Babylon from about 1000 BCE. The text focuses on epilepsy and stroke. It mentions the belief that if someone falls on his left side during an epileptic seizure or a stoke, it was because of having been struck down by the hand of the toilet demon. The translated text asserts:

> If his right side is let down: stroke (inflicted by) a lurker;
> he will recover. If the right side of his body is in its
> entirety let down: stroke (inflicted by) a lurker; he has
> been hit at the rear. (Stol, 1993)

Šulak is also referenced in Tablet XXVII of the *Babylonian Diagnostic Handbook* that gives instruction on exorcisms. The toilet demon is classified as a "lurker," which is a type of demon who patiently waits for the victim to be alone. These lurker-type demons would also wait for people in dark areas and abandoned places. This concept of a lurker, including of a demon that lurks in the toilet, waiting until you are alone and at your most vulnerable, is also found in Hittite diagnostic medical texts (ibid.). Eventually, early forms of Christianity adopted the concept of toilet demons, considering them unclean spirits that could cause physical and spiritual harm.

Egyptian Influence

As a displaced people, the Jews encountered many different beliefs and cultures, often integrating aspects of them into their own beliefs, even though they tried very hard to keep their own beliefs intact. In another case of cultural diffusion, the time the Jews spent in Egypt may have also influenced their ideas of demons. Historians and archaeologists often dispute the idea of the Jewish presence in Egypt, citing no archaeological evidence. Many scholars also find parts of the story too fantastic, like when Moses parts the Red Sea so that his people may pass through it. Additionally, archaeologists have no Egyptian primary source accounts referencing slaves, plagues, or an exodus and subsequent wandering people. However, religious scholars take the story to be true and have made some interesting connections as a result. According to some rabbinical scholars, the many demons and deities of the Egyptian pantheon influenced the Jewish people and their idea of evil.

One theory demonstrating the direct influence on the Jews in Egypt and their beliefs about Egyptian entities centers on the Passover story. After 400 years of slavery, the Jews were released from Egypt. Because the pharaoh refused to let the people go, God punished the land with ten plagues. The tenth plague was God's final judgment. The firstborns of people and animals would be killed unless the blood from a lamb was smeared on the doorframe. God sent a spirit to do the killing, but if this entity saw the blood on the doorframe, it would know to "pass over" that home because God had instructed this entity to spare the Jewish people who followed his commands.

In some cases, the entity whom God sent to kill the firstborn children is described as an angel of the lord. However, as was the tendency in those days, there was a fine line between angels and demons. Only God could command these beings to do anything. Hence, some rabbinical scholars have suggested that the entity God sent to kill the children was the Egyptian goddess Sekhmet.

Sekhmet

Just as the Sumerians had demons who represented the complexity and duality of the human experience, as well as the cosmos, the Egyptian deities were also complex. The Egyptian goddess Sekhmet was one of the fiercest Egyptian deities. She was the daughter of Ra and guardian of the sun. Sekhmet was also responsible for protecting Ma'at, the deity and embodiment of truth, order, balance, justice, love, healing, and cosmic harmony.

However, Sekhmet was also responsible for plagues, war, and destruction of humanity. In her peaceful form, she is the Egyptian goddess Hathor. As the story goes, the gods all convened in secret to meet with Ra, as he had requested. They bowed to their king and he asked them to report to him how things were on Earth. All the gods present unanimously agreed to send a punisher to kill all of humanity. Ra also agreed and sent for his daughter, Hathor. Hathor gladly obeyed him and changed into her wild form, Sekhmet, the bloodthirsty lion-headed goddess. As Sekhmet, she turned against the Egyptian people. The humans fled into the desert, trying to escape from the evil beast, as she swept through the night sky killing everyone in her path. After a day of slaughtering humankind, Ra felt compassion and thought he had punished humanity enough.

Sekhmet, also called the Eye of Ra, was drunk on the blood of humanity and uncontrollable. She would not stop until the human race was completely exterminated. Now that her strength was unleashed, Ra had to find a way to stop her. He sent messengers to Aswan that lay in the south of Egypt. They swiftly brought large quantities of red ochre, fine earth mixed with iron oxide or hematite, and then brought them to his temple in Heliopolis. The high priest was instructed to grind the hematite, and the maids had to grind enough barley to fill 7,000 jars of beer. This beer was mixed with the red ocher so that it would look like blood. Ra's team immediately went to work and toiled all night long. The human race depended on it.

Early the next morning, Ra appeared and gave the order to fill the fields where Sekhmet was last seen so that she could further satisfy her unquenchable thirst for blood with the red beer to a height of three palms. When Sekhmet woke up, she saw the fields with the red liquid and was delighted. Gluttonous, she immediately began to swallow up the beer, which she believed was more human blood. She became terribly drunk and completely forgot her mission to kill the Egyptian people. She returned to her father's palace to sleep off her drunkenness.

Ra had saved his people, and the savage goddess changed back into the peaceful Hathor. Yet, the experience was too much for Ra, and so he renounced the throne and left the responsibility to Thoth, the god of wisdom and writing. Thoth taught humankind to read and write, while Ra, with the help of his other children, ascended to heaven for a period of retirement in peace and tranquility.

Another version of this story tells that Ra punished humankind because they no longer obeyed their religious duties and did not make the prescribed sacrifices. The gods then decided to send the lion-headed goddess Sekhmet to Earth to punish humankind. However, when they saw that Sekhmet was slaughtering people and enjoying the taste of their blood, they realized that in this way humanity would be completely vanquished. So they also tricked her with a red-colored alcoholic beverage and managed to save humankind. From then on, humans learned that the gods should be taken seriously and treated with great respect. They would no longer neglect their rules and religious duties. Because of these stories, Sekhmet is sometimes called "Lady of Drunkenness."

Ammit, the Soul-Eater

Ammit, known as the "soul-eater" or "devourer," was an Egyptian personification of divine retribution for all the sins someone had committed during his life. She had an important role in weighing the heart. Ammit lived in the Hall of Ma'at, in the underworld, near the scale of justice, where the hearts of the dead were weighed by Anubis against Ma'at, the principle of truth and justice. The hearts of those who failed the test were given to Ammit to devour, and their souls were not allowed to enter the Fields of Aalu, the ideal fertile lands where the gods lived. Thus, they had to return to the realm of the living as ghosts. These ghosts were often the spirits of those who had ended their lives in miserable ways, such as being a sinner or having not reached their earthly goals. They may have also been prisoners or people who had died violently. Someone who had committed many sins was cast out, and his soul must wander around the world forever.

Ammit was not honored and was never considered a goddess. Instead, she embodied the fears of all Egyptians. She caused the people to live under the threat of eternal restlessness if they did not follow the principle of Ma'at. That is why Ammit is depicted with the head of a crocodile, the front of her body is that of a lion or leopard, and her back took the form of a hippopotamus—a combination of what the ancient Egyptians regarded as the most dangerous animals. Ammit is often described as a demon, but here again, like Sekhmet and Pazuzu, she is also considered a protector because she could defend against other entities, as well as the fact that she held an important position in maintaining justice and balance.

The ancient Egyptians believed justice and cosmic harmony could be attained through balancing its parts. Egypt was even called the Two Lands, referring to the Valley (Upper Egypt) and the

Delta (Lower Egypt). The human king would claim the title "Lord of the Two Lands," because in his role, he unified both Upper and Lower Egypt, as well as the human and the divine worlds. This unification, the balancing of all of Egypt and the cosmos, was achieved through one human figurehead: Sekhmet, the protector of justice, was the unifying force in heaven, making her the necessary balance to the king on earth. Historians often explain this double nature as stemming from the Egyptian concept of cosmic power. The ancient Egyptians believed that power had an active, positive element, as well as a passive, negative element; both needed to be balanced and brought into equilibrium by regularly appeasing the destructive negative aspect (Germond, 1982).

Ammit has many titles: soul-eater, bone-eater, devourer of the dead, devourer of millions, eater of hearts, and greatness of death. In addition to Sekhmet, she is often linked to several other gods like Tawaret, who has physically similar characteristics. Tawaret was the companion of Bes, a demon that has been a part of the archaeological record from Upper Egypt dating back to the Old Kingdom (2686–2134 BCE).

CHAPTER 3

Old-World Evil

*And I beheld another beast coming up out of the earth;
and he had two horns like a lamb, and he spake as a
dragon.*

—Rev. 13:11 (KJV)

In the iconographic development of human history, animals merged with humans to create strange hybrid creatures that, at first glance, may appear demonic. People in the protoliterate era were under considerable pressure from having to adjust from a primitive, wild existence to living together in cities. Even in modernity, with mass communication and almost instant cultural exportation, there is still a cultural disconnect between people who live in large urban centers like New York versus those in the countryside of Iowa. We cannot even imagine what it would be like to live in the protoliterate era, where people struggled to adjust from living in a Paleolithic style to an organized society with rules and customs. This adjustment period gave rise to a dualistic concept of "good versus evil" resulting from the stress and growing pains of the civilizing process: the struggle between wild man and civilized man.

Ancient literary myths contain clues to the effort to balance or resolve this duality. The *Epic of Gilgamesh,* the oldest written story known on Earth, explores complex, innately human themes like this epic struggle between wildness and civility. In 2700 BCE, the Sumerian king of Uruk, Gilgamesh, was thought to be two-thirds god and one-third human. Described as tyrannical, his people cried out to their gods for help, which resulted in the gods sending the primitive man Enkidu to befriend Gilgamesh.

Enkidu lived on the outskirts of the city; hairy and beastly in his appearance, he was depicted as an animallike man who dwelled with the four-legged beasts of the forest. In the story, he was eventually "civilized" by succumbing to the lurid seduction of a temple harlot. After he lost his primitive innocence following this experience with the prostitute, Enkidu made his way to the city of Uruk to challenge Gilgamesh to a wrestling match. Although he lost the fight, he gained the respect and friendship of the great king. The two men became friends and went on a series of epic adventures. In terms of duality, one of the main themes in the *Epic of Gilgamesh* is that of "taming" the wild. The story's theme of taming the wild is a way to express the desire for balance and deal with the discomfort of duality in the human experience.

Sumerian seals depicting beast-hero combat are a common archaeological find, supporting the idea that the people of Sumer were fixated on the beast-fight motif, also referred to as the Gilgamesh motif. Although in these representations humans were always victorious over the beast, the duality eventually blurred when depictions developed of monsters with human torsos and animal legs. The notion that man may not always win against beast emerged as a terrifying alternative. Maybe the line between wild and civil was no longer clear? When the "wild" people of the countryside began assimilating into the civilized world, did it always go smoothly? Instead of civilization winning, could these primitive aspects have invaded the city to threaten its very existence by pulling humans back to their animalistic state?

Sumerians believed that demons had both positive and negative attributes. Like Enkidu, these animal-human hybrid beings were sent by the gods to interact with humans on Earth. These monstrous representations, often in the form of statues or figurines, contributed to the development of a pantheon of demons in the early part of human civilization, as discussed in the previous chapter. When seeking to understand the role and function of evil entities to human culture, it is important to first recognize that the word "demon," from the Greek *daemon*, does not imply inherent evil, but rather a divine force. Thus, for many in the ancient world, demons served a dual function, like the destructive-yet-protective force of Pazuzu in Mesopotamia. To the Greeks, as described in the Symposium of Plato (ca. 427–ca. 347 BCE), demons are divine beings that occupy the space between the heavenly realm of gods and the earthly realm of humans, in a sort of gray area.

The contrast became more apparent to the early Christians, who routinely demonized old pagan divinities. Yet again, this narrative created an imaginary divide between primitive and modern, regression and progression. The new ways are good; the old ways are evil. Perhaps the fear was that by adopting the old ways, humanity would devolve into a chaotic natural state where mortal danger lurks around every corner. The promise of civilization, our social contract, is that we will have rights and protection. There is safety in civilization.

Medieval European artists and authors continued to link the beasts of the wild with the people of the outskirts of towns.

This contributed to a sense of "otherness," eventually building a mythos (and inevitable fear) around the folk people. They lumped their beliefs and cultural fears into a cauldron of beasts, evil, magic, and monsters. According to the Bible, man was made in the image of God himself, so by depicting demons as animal-human hybrids, medieval artists created a "bestial perversion of God's image" (Strickland, 2003).

Bes

The cool, blue moonlight poured into the open window, washing over the young woman's sweaty forearms. Shivering from both the fear of uncertainty of what was to come and the intense pains of her hard labor, she gritted her teeth and clenched every fiber of her being at the crest of each new contraction. Her tense, naked body convulsed repeatedly, well into the Egyptian night, as she squatted over the birthing bricks. She clutched a small amulet that featured a visage of a stout, hairy, human-animal effigy. The carved statuette was wet from sweaty palms, yet firmly secured to its wearer by a supple leather cord. The fifteen-year-old slave's mistress and matron of the birth arbor, only a few years her elder, washed the girl's back with a concoction made from *heqet*, a pale, light beer made with honey, and dried saffron she had just crushed in a small pestle. This was believed to help induce delivery, while also soothing the myriad of mosquito bites from earlier when the night was young. The girl's mistress encouraged her to drink the beer, as well. Her young husband tended a brazier's smoky coals just outside, where he would await the placenta for preparation of his bride's first meal as a new mother. He nervously fidgeted with his own Bes amulet beneath his heavy night cloak while trying to warm himself near the stove.

Bes was prominently displayed throughout the birth arbor, his leering grin elaborately carved into both interior and exterior wood pillars. The repulsive image of the deity's face was visible in the lamplight on everything from cosmetics cases and knife handles to hairbrushes, cameos, and baby rattles. A large stone relief of the ancient Egyptian god of fertility and protector of pregnant women, childbirth, and children stood against the east wall of the hut, facing the soon-to-be mother with its large ears and wild mane.

As the night wore on, the mistress demanded that her slave drink the saffron beer. She began to speak rhythmically in a low, barely audible, yet assertive voice. As she chanted incantations, she rocked the servant girl back and forth into a trance, invoking the spirit of Bes to enter the room and perhaps to enter the girl. If Bes possessed her, it might ensure the safe delivery of the girl's newborn. The matron, herself in a trancelike state, would rely on the magic of Bes to ward off any evil that could befall the impending birth.

Who, or what, was Bes? Bes was an ancient Egyptian god of both war and fertility and was especially known as a protector of women and children, above all others. He is often described as a bestial, dwarfish demon or god and is generally associated with sexuality, humor, and celebration, including drinking and merriment. Some archaeologists have suggested that Bes was not a deity of Egyptian origin but perhaps adopted from the folklore of slaves taken from farther south on the African continent. Inscriptions found accompanying Bes artifacts frequently mentioned that he came from "the Divine Land." It could be that his image represents, not a dwarf or troll-like figure, but that of a lion-human hybrid, possibly rearing on hind legs. The name "Bes" may be a derivative of an ancient African word for cat (*besa*); however, his name could also link him to Bast, the cat goddess, which might have accounted for his feline strength and power. The demon is part of the archaeological record from Upper Egypt dating back to the Old Kingdom (2686–2134 BCE), which suggests that Bes may very well have been of Egyptian origin, but so far, there is insufficient evidence to support either origin theory.

Bes was somewhat unique among ancient Egyptian deities in that unlike other gods such as Isis, Horus, or Osiris, Bes was not associated with formal temples, except for one designated to protect the vineyards at the oasis of el-Bahariya, in the Western Desert of Egypt, and no priests were known to worship him. Bes was one of the only ancient Egyptian deities to be primarily portrayed in paintings, carvings, reliefs, and sculpture face-front, instead of the typical side-profile portrayals of the other gods. Bes was perhaps the most popular god among ancient Egyptians of all classes. This reverence may actually have been due to his lack of royal and religious sanctioning. Bes was regarded as a kind, benevolent god who was seen as a protector of the weak and an enemy of evil, but with a lighthearted side that was interested in pleasure and mischief. His spirit and magic were mostly invoked during labor and birth. His image was used to decorate a great many personal and household items, which resulted in a proliferation of thousands of Bes artifacts in museums all over the world today. Toward the end of his popularity, between 300 BCE and approximately 30 BCE, Bes objects were traded all across the ancient Mediterranean world. Local artisans and craftsmen outside of Egypt produced objects that featured Bes for Phoenician, Cypriot, Greek, and Roman enthusiasts.

Amulets and personal items depicting Bes were popular for more than two thousand years. The archaeological record even shows that some women decorated their bodies with his image.

Women who were experiencing difficulties getting pregnant may have even had images of Bes with an erect penis tattooed on their bodies to promote fertility while sacred prostitutes may have tattooed his image near their pubic areas or inner thighs to protect against venereal diseases. His role as a warrior and protector was embraced by the Roman Empire. Roman soldiers were known to drink from goblets decorated with Bes portrayed as a legionnaire and would inscribe images of Bes on the insides of their shields before battle. The fascination with this god finally waned, but ultimately survived well into the new millennium (CE), leaving its mark in culture as recently as the reign of Constantine the Great (ca. 300–325 CE).

Pan

Can you imagine hearing, or even feeling, a sound so horrific and terrifying that it might cause you to panic? How might that sound? A piercing shriek? A guttural roar? An ear-splitting, rasping grind, like divine nails raking an Olympic chalkboard? Perhaps an ominous vibration so deep that your intestines feel it more than your ears can hear it? Although we can never be certain what it sounded like, the ancient Greek god Pan was known to have been able to produce such terrible vocalizations as to induce mighty giants to flee in their battles with the gods. According to legend, Pan actually visited the Athenian runner Pheidippides during his famous journey to Sparta prior to the Battle of Marathon (490 BCE) after which a mighty bellow attributed to Pan caused *panikos* (literally, "the fear caused by Pan," from which the word "panic" is derived) among the invading Persians. This action allegedly caused the invaders to abandon their first attempt to conquer Athens and instead flee for their lives, withdrawing to their ships anchored in the bay of Marathon. It is said that the outnumbered Athenians used Pan's scream as a battle cry that emboldened them to attack and rout the retreating Persians, slaughtering large numbers of Persian soldiers before they could reach the harbor.

Like his Egyptian contemporary Bes, Pan was an ancient therianthropic (combination of both human and animal elements) deity of uncertain origins. Also like Bes, Pan represented a primitive, wild nature and was associated with the pleasures of life—notably, wine, sex, music, and mischief. Similarly to Bes, Pan was a lusty demon with a voracious appetite for frolicking with both human men and women, nymphs and goddesses, as well as goats and sheep, and was thus associated with sexuality and fertility. Pan was the spirit of the untamed, and again, like Bes, was beloved by the people, in spite of his ugly and animalistic form.

The horned god is often regarded in modernity as a joyful sprite, frequently depicted as dancing and playing his syrinx (panpipes or pan flute), named for a nymph pursued by Pan who was changed into hollow reeds by her sisters near a riverbank in order to escape him, from which Pan crafted his instrument. This archetypal image appears in ancient Greek artifacts, beginning around 500 BCE as a playful goat rearing on hind legs, but it only denotes a portion of Pan's varied nature. In later red-figure pottery scenes, Pan was painted as the half-man, half-beast character with which we're familiar, showing the god with a human head and torso, but with ram- or goatlike horns and ears and fur-covered legs ending in cloven hooves, holding his famous reed flute.

Pan.

The modern translation for the word "Pan" is "everything" or "all-encompassing," hence terms such as "Pan-American," which means "all of the Americas." The ancient god was immensely popular, and his name affirmed his reach—Pan seemed to be everywhere. Paradoxically, Pan was not sanctioned by the keepers of the gods, nor did he enjoy temples in his honor or devoted clergy to sing his praises. Pan was not worshipped in the settled areas of the Greek city-states by scholars and philosophers in the ways that other Greek gods, such as Zeus, Hera, Athena, or Apollo were. The pagan deity was instead cherished and adored by the rural people of the countryside: the shepherds, hunters, farmers, and common folk at the fringes of civilized Greek society who viewed him as their guardian. Pan's worship began in Arcadia, the sparsely populated and wild, mountainous province from where he supposedly hailed. Rather than temples, remote caves and grottoes were often used as places to worship Pan, along with a cadre of woodland and water nymphs. The archaeological record shows that shepherds, in particular, were known to have left sacrifices of slaughtered goats and kids (young goats), along with vases, lamps, and reed flutes, among other things, in his honor. It is written that honey, milk, and garlands of pine were also offered. Pan was so beloved that his image was even struck on the reverse side of certain Arcadian coins by 360 BCE. After his association with the victory at Marathon against the Persians, Pan was fully immortalized with a dedication at the Acropolis at Athens.

The horned god's connection to ideas of pastoral living, naturalism, and the pursuit of creativity and the arts represents the innocent side of his dual nature. Throughout the centuries, Pan's darker, more sinister side became an equally enduring part of his character. In the new millennium, Plutarch (46–120 CE), the first century Greek biographer and essayist, recounted an extraordinary event in his famous work, *Moralia,* of an apparently divine voice that declared that the great Pan was dead (Plutarch and Babbitt, 2005). In the second century CE, Greek geographer and author Pausanias noted in his ten-volume *Description of Greece* that he still observed active shrines to Pan in sacred caves throughout the countryside. After the Council of Nicaea issued its creed and established the Roman Catholic Church in the beginning of the fourth century CE, the demonization of Pan was in full swing. Early Christian theologians sought to portray Pan not as an impish, nature-loving being of antiquity, but as an animalistic, evil embodiment of the Devil. Augustine (Saint Augustine, 354–430 CE) was a fourth-century Christian ecclesiastic philosopher and theologian who wrote that "sylvans and fauns [satyrs, such as Pan], who are commonly called 'incubi,' had often made wicked assaults upon women, and satisfied their lust upon them" (Dods, 1878).

Pan's horns, cloven hooves, and wild appearance proved to be the archetypal form attributed to unholy demons and devils as the Church engaged in the widespread transformation of pagan Europe to Christianity. The pagans were initially unwilling to accept that the ways of life to which they were accustomed, which included unrestrained sexuality, violence, and polytheism, were then deemed sinful. Among its tools to coerce the people to reject their primitive cultures and to embrace the relative confinements of Christianity, the Church employed a strategy of using the fear of eternal damnation and suffering at the clawed hands of nightmarish, horned beasts. As Pan came to embody Satan and his minions, the Church had a frightening visual manifestation to illustrate what happens to the sexually immoral, uncivilized, and unrepentant.

Cernunnos

As early as seven centuries before Christ, an inspired pagan artist carved an image of a giant stag-headed god into a glacially smoothed rock face in the northern Italian Alps. The being in the ancient petroglyph is portrayed standing, covered in a long, full-body garment, with tall, spiky antlers atop its head. Many scholars agree that this carving represents what is perhaps the earliest known artifact of the Celtic god Cernunnos, a primitive lord of forests, nature, and fertility. The antlered deity depicted in this early form was a western and central European Bronze Age contemporary of the Egyptian Bes and Greek Pan, and occupied a similar role in its Celtic pantheon to its pagan worshippers.

Horned God Cernunnos.

The ancient Celts who lived in what are present-day northern Italy, Austria, Germany, France, and Spain were polytheists who worshipped and revered a wide variety of gods and goddesses related to nature and the environment. Centered in temperate Europe, the Celts were divided into tribes and clans who shared distinct values during an era referred to the La Tène culture (ca. 800 BCE–50 CE), named for the archaeological site of La Tène, in present-day Switzerland. Celtic artifacts from this Iron Age period tend to be characterized by ornate decoration featuring curved, swirled, and elaborately twisted elements, particularly in metalwork. The word "Celt" is derived from the Greek *Keltoi*, meaning "barbarian," a reflection of how they were perceived by the ancient Greeks, and later, the Romans.

The history of the Celts is sketchy as they had no written language, but historians tend to agree that based on styles and distribution of certain La Tène-style artifacts at least some Celtic tribal chiefs may have traded with the Greeks during the sixth century BCE. By the early third century BCE, the Celtic tribes were facing threats to their homelands from marauding Germanic tribes who were expanding their ranges south into the Alpine forests and north in southern Scandinavia. During these years, the Celts themselves expanded their range, migrated farther west, settled deeper into the Iberian Peninsula and eventually crossed the English Channel and became the dominant people of the British Isles. In the fourth century BCE, Celtic expansion through the Alps and into northern Italy led Celtic warriors into violent confrontations with Etruscan and Roman societies. In approximately 387/386 BCE, the young and vulnerable city-state of Rome was sacked by the Senones, one of many Gallic (the Celtic people who inhabited Gaul, the area of present-day France) tribes that would engage in war with the Romans during the series of Roman-Gallic Wars.

Workers harvesting dried peat in 1891 discovered what would become the largest piece of European silver metalwork to have survived from the Iron Age. The Gundestrup Cauldron was found, dismantled into five pieces, in the bog Rævemosen at Gundestrup, Jutland (in present-day Himmerland, Denmark). Scholars tend to agree that the reassembled cauldron, with its ornately decorated cylindrical side plates and spherical base, was likely a valuable religious vessel from the second or first century BCE. A paleobotanical investigation of the bog determined that the surrounding land was likely dry when the pieces of the cauldron were stacked together in an apparent attempt to hide it, and that the peat bog formed after the vessel was left, surrounding and encapsulating it for the ages. The artifact is renowned for Plate A, which features a depiction of the antlered lord of the forest, seated with a horned serpent in his left hand and surrounded by other mysterious animals observing him from all sides.

Only one Gaulish artifact has ever been recovered that actually names the god. During excavation of the soil amid the construction of a new crypt deep beneath the famed medieval Notre-Dame Cathedral in Paris on March 6, 1710, the jagged remnants of a strange, esoteric limestone pillar were unearthed. The badly damaged *Pilier des Nautes* (Pillar of the Boatmen) is a carved stone column featuring bas-reliefs of a number of Roman and Celtic deities. Broken and incomplete, the totem appears to have been dedicated to Roman emperor Tiberius by the local guild of merchant sailors of the Seine sometime in the first century CE and seems to emphasize the somewhat uneasy merging of Gallo-Roman cultures. The pillar includes the engraved name [C]ERNVNNOS (the *C* is mostly missing now due to damage) over the image of the antlered god, which is depicted with two large torques suspended from juvenile stag antlers. (A torque, also spelled "torc" or "torq," is a large metal ring that was twisted into shape from either a single piece or from separate strands of usually gold, silver, bronze, or copper. These were generally worn around the necks of high-ranking Iron Age Celtic men.)

At the dawn of the new millennium, the Roman Empire continued to expand its range north and west, conquering territories held by Celts and other barbaric tribes. Celtic settlements, forts, and farming villages were often burned or destroyed and the Celtic people on the Continent were subjugated, enslaved, or killed. Celtic culture was diminished and absorbed by the Romans; the physical ruins of their societies—buildings, bridges, and other structures—were generally constructed of organic materials such as wood and thatch and were fittingly reclaimed by nature. The remnants of the Celtic culture were pushed to the frontiers of the Roman Empire until Rome no longer deemed them threatening. Only the Celts living in the far northern and western fringes of the British Isles, north of Hadrian's Wall in northern England, or in Ireland, where Rome never set foot, were able to escape Roman subjugation. Their culture continued to thrive beyond the end of Roman influence and the advent of Christianity, and these Celts continued to hold fast to their pagan ways centuries into the Common Era, exalting and revering their many gods and goddesses, including Cernunnos—*the horned one.*

The Descent of the Pagan Gods

By the middle of the fifth century BCE, the Roman Empire had withdrawn from Britain, overwhelmed by repeated invasions from Scottish Picts and Irish warriors from the north and west, and Anglo-Saxons from the east and south. Romano-British civilization crumbled into chaos as Britain entered the Dark Ages (476–800 CE). The European continent experienced a similar era of intellectual and civil darkness during the early medieval period. Waves of barbaric tribes, including Huns, Goths, Vandals, and Franks, engaged in battles for dominance in the vacuum left by the absence of Roman rule. This age of anarchy lasted over three centuries, until the reign of Charlemagne I (800–814 CE) brought a new sense of order to western Europe and fully enthroned the Holy Roman Empire. The Roman Catholic Church engaged in a campaign of papal missions to restore civility and order through the widespread conversion of pagans to Christianity.

Perhaps the most infamous of these missionaries was Saint Patrick, the patron saint of Ireland, who arrived in 448 CE from Britain to establish Christianity as the official religion. The man we know as Saint Patrick was likely named Magonus Saccatus Patricius when he was captured as a fourteen-year-old boy on the west coast of Roman Britannia (present-day Wales) by seaborne Irish pirates and brought to Ireland as a slave. The fog of myth regarding the folkloric hero obscures the boundaries between historical fact and legend, but he is celebrated for ultimately converting the last of the Irish pagans to Christianity. Aside from his infamous exploits of driving all of the snakes from Ireland (a complete fabrication because no snakes have lived on the island since the last period of glaciation), several other direct confrontations with the pagan underworld are attributed to Patrick. In one such tale, he used his apostolic staff to kill the evil hag Garravogue by splitting her into multiple parts. In another, he battled a serpentine water monster called Caoránach submerged beneath the waters of Lough Derg after she swallowed him whole. He emerged victorious two days later, having cut his way out from her belly with his crosier, and his bloody massacre of the beast made the water red, hence the meaning of the name, "dark, red lake." To this day, there is a Christian pilgrimage site in Lough Derg in County Donegal (Ulster Province) called Station Island where a large, pitted stone now known as the Altar of Confession is said to be the ancient skeleton of the demon Caoránach. Another legend depicts Patrick battling the sky demon Corra, the mother of the Devil and all demons, at the top of Croagh Patrick, the triangular mountain that today bears his name. He purportedly threw a divinely powerful bell at her, striking her from the sky, then threw her body into Lough na Corra, a lake at the base of the mountain where she drowned.

It's interesting to note that many of the pagan gods and goddesses that Patrick demonized and eventually killed were serpentine, dragon-like beasts in a land that never knew snakes. Perhaps these legends provided the symbolic figures necessary for the Church to rebuke in the form of serpents, which could be portrayed as frightening and demonic, rather than condemning benevolent goddesses who were once honored by the people the Church wished to convert.

During the period of the High Middle Ages (ca. 1000–1350 CE), much of Europe was firmly in the grip of feudalism and absorbed into Christendom. The Church's influence and affiliation with elite families, landholders, and monarchs led to its domination of the largely poor and illiterate masses. Part of the Church's strategy to reform pagans involved the widespread demonization of their formerly beloved deities. One such being that was made wicked by the Church was the pooka (Irish: *púca, phouka;* English: *pouke, puck;* Welsh: *pwca;* Dutch: *puki*). Like other friendly and familiar figures of the Celtic folklore of the British Isles and the Netherlands, the pooka was rather easily reimagined as a grotesque, goblin-like demon that haunted the pagan countryside, terrorizing souls who had not yet accepted Christ as their lord. Some legends portray the pooka as a shape-shifting specter that could appear as a wild white horse or a large and mysterious black dog, but with later Christian influence, the impish creature was often seen as a diminutive devil, with goatish horns and clawed hands.

The demonized tales of pookas allegorically reflected the Christian method of conversion from pagan to Christian beliefs and values. A typical yarn might describe pookas coming down from the mountains at night and randomly selecting the home of a peasant family to cause mischief with; generally, the homes of nonbelievers. Versions of a common cautionary tale described the discovery of work being done overnight around the farmhouse, including washing and mending clothing; the mending of hedges and homes; and the care of livestock, such as milking, grooming, and the gathering of eggs. These acts of perceived kindness represented the myopic, pagan views of the gods and goddesses of old, but the stories took a darker turn; dealings with the pooka became terrifying pacts with evil. To repay the pooka, members of the family would leave gifts for them each night for the previous night's work. These gifts may have included bowls of buttermilk, baked breads, cheese, turnips, or berries in season. The pooka accepted the gifts and continued their deeds every night hence, until someone, usually a child, either forgot, or worse, decided to drink the buttermilk or eat the bread. In these stories, acts of deceit against the pooka usually resulted in them ceasing their work. When the family would attempt to restart the cycle with a new night of gifts, the pooka would change from mere mischievous sprites to frightful devils, hell-bent on cruel acts of vengeance. The pooka were believed to have exacted heavy tolls against the people who broke their arrangements. They were blamed for crop failures and livestock deaths, fires, and missing people. They were also known to have waged campaigns of misery and suffering upon their victims by reversing the progress of hard work. These acts may have included the filling in of hand-dug ditches or wells; theft or poisoning of eggs, milk, and cheese; the tearing down of stone walls; or the dethatching of roofing materials. The torment would continue until it abruptly ended, often when the family sought relief from the nearest pastor.

Our knowledge of pookas and other later Celtic beings comes mainly from oral tradition, but as medieval Europe moved further toward the Renaissance, we see the rise of Gothic architecture in the High Middle Ages (ca. 1000–1350 CE) and the accompanying carved stone demons that we typically call gargoyles. The feudal system, fully established and supported by the Church, brought a degree of order and civility to the land, and the Holy Roman Empire was never stronger. Christendom continued its mission of bringing pagans into the fold while collecting tithes, which supported building brigades of European Crusaders, controlled by papal military leaders from Rome. Christian armies won territory from the Muslims, both in the

Middle East and, especially, in Moorish Spain. By-products of the Crusades and the increased interaction with the Muslim world included a renewed emphasis on learning, particularly in the areas of science, mathematics, and medicine. Rome also controlled and dominated Mediterranean trade, which further helped to improve medieval Europe's economic fortunes. The Church devoted many of its new resources to the construction of soaring cathedrals, monasteries, and universities all across Europe. The places of learning were generally reserved for nobility, monks, clergy, and other devout Christians. Peasants and other common people remained mostly illiterate, but there was an increase in the numbers of artisans and tradesmen who were skilled and capable of building grandiose, highly adorned cathedrals. These structures were by far the most important buildings in medieval culture, and they were the largest buildings in any town. The spires of Gothic cathedrals stood above the treetops to form the earliest urban skylines. Gothic architecture evolved from late Romanesque beginnings, combined with the Church's attention to decorative details, such as flying buttresses, high-pointed arches, beautifully painted stained-glass windows, and horrific gargoyles and grotesques. These stone creatures provide us with archaeological evidence to support our understanding of the Church's war on paganism.

The term "gargoyle," strictly speaking, refers to decorative spouts that serve the single purpose of diverting rain and snow-melt from parapet gutters, away from stonework and masonry, in order to preserve it. The word derives from the Old French *gargole,* or *gargoule,* which means "throat." The sound made by these sculptural waterspouts after a rain is also where the word "gargle" originates. Although we tend to refer to any sculpted beasts on building exteriors as gargoyles, the correct term for these ornamental caricatures is "grotesques."

A seventh-century account from Rouen, a Norman village along the River Seine in northern France, describes the exploits of Saint Romanus and his battle against La Gargouille, a terrible dragon that wreaked havoc in the countryside. The pagans who lived near the town described the beast as having a long, reptilian neck and wild eyes, horns, and wicked teeth. The dragon, a minion of Satan himself, tormented the people when they approached the river by spewing jets of water or fire from his mouth at them, then devouring the villagers before they could recover and escape. The townspeople began a ritual to placate the dragon by offering a human sacrifice each year. It is said that although La Gargouille preferred undefiled maidens, the villagers would instead offer criminals and thieves.

The dragon's onslaughts did not stop, and finally, Romanus, the archbishop of Rouen at the time, determined that he could end the dragon's reign of terror. He promised the people that he could eliminate La Gargouille if they accepted Christ, abandoned their pagan ways, and promised to be baptized and build a church. Armed only with a crucifix and assisted only by an imprisoned criminal, Romanus went to the dragon's lair and proceeded to draw him out. Legend has it that La Gargouille emerged from the Seine and immediately moved to attack the bishop, who subdued the monster with the power of the cross, compelling the tamed demon to walk to the center of the town on its own accord, where the villagers proceeded to kill and burn the condemned creature. When the pyre finally extinguished, and the people of Rouen cast the ash pile into the river to wash it away, they discovered that the head and neck did not burn as it was tempered to withstand its own fiery breath. The legend goes on to say that the flame-hardened shell of the head and neck was the final detail to be affixed to the new church, where it endured as a peaceful water-spout and symbol that Christ's death defeated evil.

Archaeologists and historians tend to believe that the widespread use of grotesques and gargoyles as elements on cathedrals and churches served a number of purposes for the Church, beginning with the practical function of water displacement. Another theory suggests that grotesques on churches and cathedrals served as apotropaic instruments, intended to ward off evil beings or harmful influences, in much the same way that superstitious people might use amulets, tokens, or good luck charms. It is also widely believed that many grotesques and gargoyles became hideous manifestations of fearsome, demonic beings in order to plainly demonstrate to a largely illiterate population that the powers of evil exist and are present outside of the church walls.

By the eleventh century, carved stone hags known as Sheela-na-Gigs appeared as grotesques over church entrances, as well as on castles and other structures, homes, and embedded into rock walls across the British Isles and western and central Europe. The highest concentration of the primitive female figures was found in Ireland and Great Britain, in Christianized areas of Anglo-Norman conquest. They were deemed ugly and somewhat frightening, often naked with no hair, breasts, or other features typically associated with feminine beauty. Most of these lewd carvings displayed bawdy grins while obscenely spreading their oversized vulva with their fingers. The Sheela-na-Gigs are thought to have represented pagan fertility goddesses, co-opted by the Church, as an attempt to sway the devotions of their followers toward Christ. Some scholars believe that the Sheelas, most of which date to the eleventh and twelfth centuries, were actually Christian creations to demonstrate the evil and ugliness of lusty, sinful females who engage in reckless and unchaste behavior.

With the passage of time, medieval gargoyles and grotesques became more elaborate, and the features of the beasts grew increasingly intricate and menacing. During the height of the Gothic movement in the High Middle Ages, gargoyles looked less like traditional animals, such as lions, and more like bizarre demons with beaks, horns, teeth, and unsettling eyes that unblinkingly glared. Gargoyles and grotesques became high art of their own accord, and no cathedral was complete without a horde of stone chimeras to invoke the fear of hell.

Centuries later, many Gothic gargoyles and grotesques have suffered the ravages of time. Although carved from limestone and marble, their high medieval–era features have largely eroded: Faces have relaxed; grimaces have softened. Many true Gothic gargoyles—elongated, horizontal waterspouts from the Middle Ages—have failed, ending up as chunks of broken limestone after falling from their perches. Plenty of actual medieval grotesques persist; however, many of the gargoyles that we see today are replacements from the Gothic Revival period of the eighteenth and nineteenth centuries. Perhaps the most famous of these are the *chimères*, the archetypal gargoyles of the Notre-Dame Cathedral in Paris.

When Victor Hugo wrote *The Hunchback of Notre Dame* in 1831, the great medieval house of God was already crumbling at nearly five hundred years old. The French novelist set his story during the reign of Louis XI in 1482, and it showcased his admiration for the cathedral and Gothic architecture in general. Centuries of exposure to the elements have eroded the stonework. The structure has endured riots and revolutions, two world wars, and decades of Parisian automobile exhaust fumes. Most of the original gargoyles were damaged or destroyed during the ravages of rioting Huguenots in the mid-sixteenth century because they believed them to be idolatrous. The cathedral and its architectural treasures were further vandalized during the French Revolution in 1793 when it was rededicated to state-sponsored atheistic cults. Just over fifty years later, French architect Eugène

Viollet-le-Duc, inspired by Hugo's book, initiated a large-scale restoration project for the Gothic church in 1845 that included his reimagining of the gargoyles. Today, his chimeras are world renowned and ironically considered the archetypes of Gothic gargoyles. In 1854, French artist and etcher Charles Méryon created a series of etchings that featured prominent views of Paris. One of his pieces captured a particular beast overlooking the city, which he named *Le Stryge* (The Vampire), making Viollet-le-Duc's horned demon perhaps the most famous grotesque ever.

Le Stryge, Notre-Dame de Paris.

After 126 years of construction, the Lincoln Cathedral in Lincoln, England, finally surpassed the Great Pyramid of Giza to stand as the tallest building in the world for the next 238 years (1311–1549 CE). It held that lofty title until its central spire collapsed in 1549 and was not rebuilt. The cathedral's timber roof was ravaged by fire in 1124. In April of 1185, much of the original church was destroyed by one of the largest earthquakes (approximately 5.0 on the Richter scale) ever recorded in Britain, yet the cathedral has endured the centuries. The Lincoln Cathedral still houses one of the four remaining exemplifications (official transcripts) of the original Magna Carta, but it may actually be better known for its mysterious demon, the Lincoln imp.

There are many accounts of the origin of the Lincoln imp, but most of them begin with Satan sending two of his demons with great winds to cause mayhem and suffering at places of worship. According to legends, the newly spawned imps first arrived in Chesterfield, England, sometime in the thirteenth or fourteenth century, and attacked the Parish Church of Saint Mary. It is said that the Devil, together with his imps, violently twisted the spire into a grotesquely distorted shape, where it stands to this day as the Crooked Spire of Chesterfield. From there, the little devils, without their master, continued on to Lincoln, where they rode the strong west winds and blew open the great doors to continue their wrath and destruction. Once inside, the beasts chased and tormented the clergy, who hid themselves to avoid injury or death. As the pastors prayed for mercy, the imps vandalized the sanctuary, overturned and smashed furniture, ripped and scattered hymnal pages, slashed candles, and broke stained-glass windows. While they were wreaking havoc, an angel appeared and ordered them to cease their evil actions. One of the imps, fearful of the angel, hid beneath the altar until it could escape the building. The other demon, bolder and perhaps more wicked, directly challenged the angel. After throwing rocks and other items at the heavenly spirit, the imp climbed a Gothic column, found a comfortable place in an ornate, V-shaped crevice of the capital at the top of the column, then crossed its leg and took a seat, where it promptly launched a barrage of blasphemous insults. The angel turned the horned creature to stone at once, where it remains today. It is still rumored that even on calm days, the spirit of the second imp continues to move around the outside of the cathedral, causing persistently windy conditions while looking for its companion.

From Old-World Gods to Demons

Bes, Pan, Cernunnos, and other bestial figures, however wild and strange they may appear to our modern eyes, were idolized, revered, and even worshipped for centuries in the Old World. These icons were closely tied to the natural world of the pagans, and they represented the mysteries of everyday life, as well as answered questions about birth, fertility, food and hunting, war, suffering, and death.

Animal-human hybridized beings have been depicted throughout the archaeological record, from Paleolithic cave paintings to Iron Age metalwork. With the rise of the Abrahamic religions, the kingdoms of the Mediterranean and Roman Europe sought economic prosperity through increased exploration and trade. Prosperity requires civility, and the planners of the nascent Holy Roman Empire knew that the tribes of central and western Europe, whom they considered barbaric and therefore uncivilized, would prove to be obstacles to development and formidable opponents until they could learn to accept—*and fear*—Christ. The task of converting hundreds of thousands of polytheistic rural and provincial people to Christianity was an enormous undertaking, but one that was necessary for the growth of peace and eventual prosperity. The Christians needed powerful tools to help with this process, which began nearly one thousand years before Gutenberg's invention of the printing press. Fear was, and is, a supremely powerful motivator, and the Church learned early that the demonization of pagan deities as evil, malevolent figures capable of creating pain, suffering, and death would be among the quickest conversion methods among the masses. Reimagining pagan gods and goddesses as bestial devils—humanoid monsters with horrible, chimeric animal features such as teeth, claws, hooves, and horns—was a relatively easy way to induce fear and inspire people to seek salvation from their pagan ways.

Evil is essentially the opposite of good. Thus, the demons of the Old World are the visual manifestation of all that is evil: minions of Satan. Demons, devils, and their old-world ilk, including goblins, imps, vampires, shape-shifters, and witches, represent a Christian view of what constitutes evil and the punishing forces that await those who reject salvation through Christ.

CHAPTER 4

Ritual Human Sacrifice

As Christianity tried to assert its dominance over the religions of the ancient world, the literal demonization of all things pagan continued as the Spanish sent ships west to conquer the New World. Upon arriving, the Spanish were amazed and horrified by what they discovered. For sixteenth-century Christians, an encounter with a culture whose gods demanded human sacrifice and mass bloodshed confirmed their belief in evil.

During a meeting between Cortes and Montezuma, Montezuma took Cortes to the pyramid of the war god on whose summit thousands of victims had died a gory death, their hearts cut out. When Cortes entered the pyramid's chamber, the first thing he noticed was the disgusting smell of rotted flesh. As his eyes got used to the dim lighting, he noticed crusty bloodstains on the walls. The glint of precious stone caught his eye. He looked over to see the eyes of the Aztec war god staring at him. The statue sat with a golden bow and arrow, and in front of him was a brazier full of human hearts, still warm. Cortes looked at Montezuma and asked him how such a great and intelligent leader such as he could believe in these treacherous gods. He explained that these so-called gods were evil demons, then asked Montezuma for permission to put a cross and a picture of the Virgin Mary inside the chamber. Montezuma took great offense at this and told Cortes that if he had known he would be so insulting to the gods, he never would have brought him to the chamber. Montezuma explained that the Aztecs believed that the gods were good because they bring health, harvests, and water. His people must offer blood sacrifices as payment for their good fortunes. Such a culture clash, to say the least. In Cortes's mind, the Christian God gave his blood to redeem mankind for their sins, whereas the Aztecs must give their blood to redeem the gods.

In Tenochtitlán, they offered people to all kinds of gods, but particularly the sun god, Huitzilopochtli. Prisoners of war were placed on a large sacrificial stone and their hearts were cut out; sometimes, the victim was decapitated. Archaeologists have discovered evidence of human sacrifice at the foot of the Templo Mayor, the primary temple of the Aztecs in what is now Mexico City. The rituals took place approximately five hundred years ago. At the site, researchers found a broken skull of a young prisoner of war who was beheaded in honor of the gods. The skull was in a vase. Further excavations are planned to determine if this was a single offering, or if it was part of a larger ceremony.

The Templo Mayor was the most important religious, political, and economic center of the Aztec capital, Tenochtitlán. The temple went through various stages of expansion until its destruction by the Spanish in 1521. The temple was site to macabre rituals wherein the Aztecs held their greatest ceremonies. In the temple, a special sacrificial stone, along with at least fifty skulls and more than two hundred jawbones were found. The skulls and bones are from men and women who ranged in age between twenty and thirty-five. According to archaeologists, the victims were beheaded on the sacrificial stone, after which their heads were used in ceremonies. Five of the skulls were buried beneath the sacrificial stone, and the other ones lay in a pile on top of it. The skulls under the stone had large holes at the temples, so they could be exhibited next to the Templo Mayor on a *tzompantli,* a huge wooden rack that held many skulls, resembling an abacus from hell. Some of the forty-five skulls found on the sacrificial stone were processed into macabre skull masks.

Skull wall in Templo Mayor, Mexico City. The main temple of the Aztecs in their capital city of Tenochtitlán.

According to the monk Diego Durán, the Aztecs sacrificed no fewer than eighty thousand people during one ceremony in 1487. Historians say this number is exaggerated and estimate that there were about five hundred to seven hundred casualties per year, perhaps twenty thousand on special occasions. To a lesser extent, the Mayans and the Incas also offered human sacrifices. Neither cultures spared the children, as they were sacrificed in both. On the people of Mesoamerica, Franciscan missionary and early ethnographer Bernardino de Sahagún wrote:

> It is certainly a matter of great wonderment that, for so
> many centuries, our Lord God has concealed a forest of
> so many idolatrous peoples whose luxuriant fruits only
> the demon harvested and holds hoarded in the infernal
> fire. Nor can I believe that the church of God would
> not be successful where the synagogue of Satan has
> had so much success, in accordance with that [phrase]
> of St. Paul's, Grace will abound where transgression
> abounded. (Jaquith, 1983)

Although the Aztecs are known for their large-scale human sacrifices, sometimes offering thousands of people in a matter of days, it may come as a surprise that most civilizations had some form of human sacrifice. Archaeological and historical evidence show that human sacrifice occurred in such places as the Mediterranean in antiquity, China until the Shang Dynasty, the Dogon in Africa and in the kingdom of Dahomey, even in modernity, in the northeast of India.

In ancient Egypt, evidence of human sacrifice can be traced to the First Dynasty, particularly during the reign of Hor-Aha, the second pharaoh of the First Dynasty. Archaeologists have found line drawings of a human sacrifice from the time of the Egyptian king Djer. Scholars have not reached a consensus on the specific reason for human sacrifice during the dynastic period. It remains a mystery.

Human sacrifices can be distinguished from each other in two ways. The first type is the cult sacrifice in which people are sacrificed as part of a temple cult. Often these are enemies or criminals, but there is also an example from the time of Pharaoh Amenhotep II in which seven Syrian princesses were ritually executed. Research has shown that around the Twenty-sixth Dynasty, cult sacrifices were replaced by wax statuettes that were burned. There is no concrete evidence for this, however, as the artifacts would have surely melted. Another type of human sacrifice is a retainer sacrifice, the killing of servants or other subordinates and then burying them with their pharaohs. The Egyptians believed that even after death, a pharaoh needed his servants and courtiers.

The royal tombs from the First Dynasty in Abydos show signs that this happened on a large scale at the time. Aha is the first pharaoh in whom this was observed, and from the First Dynasty, all his successors also performed retainer sacrifice. Around the burial buildings and the mortuary temples there are long rows of small trenches in which wooden boxes are located. These held hundreds of people, many of whom were women. Recent research shows that these people were probably killed by strangulation or possibly poison; however, archaeologists do not agree on many aspects of these sacrifices.

Historians theorize that these retainer sacrifices ended due to an increased demand for luxury goods and services. The Egyptians could no longer waste important human capital, especially when they considered the huge loss of talented, well-trained, and experienced craftsmen. No longer was it acceptable to kill off the elite's most talented artisans and career professionals. Can you imagine if we did this now? What if Jeff Bezos died, and as a result, all the people who work for Amazon, everyone from accountants to distribution center employees, would also have to die? Of course, the scale is clearly disproportionate, but it is similarly mind-boggling. In the years that followed, the servants were replaced by wooden models and figurines in the tombs as symbolic substitutes for the retainer sacrifices. These figures have been discovered in a majority of private graves, leading some to suggest that they may have served a different purpose. As with many aspects of history, debates are ongoing, and mysteries remain unsolved.

The Abrahamic religions, though, rejected the ritual sacrifice of people. Jews, Christians, and Muslims believe that Abraham was instructed by God to sacrifice his only son, Isaac, but he was stopped at the last moment by an angel of God. The reason God gave that order is in Genesis 22:12, namely, to test whether Abraham was obedient. This was a true a test of faith and obedience because Moses had instructed the Israelites to reject the practice of child sacrifice. The Book of Leviticus strongly condemns this practice in many verses, as does the rest of the Old Testament. Thus, Abraham had to trust that it was indeed the one true God who had commanded him to kill his own son.

Archaeologists discovered thousands of urns containing the cremated remains of children during the excavation of the Sanctuary of Tinit in Carthage. Researchers determined that all of the children found had been born prematurely and were then gathered, burned, and sacrificed to the gods. In Carthage, they shared the beliefs and practices of the Canaanites and Phoenicians, who continued the practice of human sacrifice until about the fifth century BCE. Archaeological excavations show that Canaanite children were burned on an altar between the ages of three and twelve months. Deuteronomy 12:31 mentions how Canaanites used to burn their children alive as a sacrifice for their gods. This practice of bringing child sacrifices is repeatedly prohibited in the Old Testament: "And thou shalt not let any of thy seed pass through the fire to Moloch, neither shalt thou profane the name of thy God: I am the Lord" (Leviticus 18:21 KJV). Who was Moloch? According to biblical tradition, Moloch (sometimes spelled Molech) was a deity worshipped in the Canaan region, inextricably linked to child sacrifice. Moloch, meaning "king," was the idol personification also linked to Baal.

In exchange for prosperity, the monstrous Moloch/Baal/Kronos/Saturn personification demanded the blood of child sacrifices, as well as the tears of mothers and fathers. The idol of Moloch was a huge brass figure seated in a brass throne with the body of a man and the head of a calf wearing a crown. Its stomach was a furnace, hollow and divided into seven compartments, each meant to receive a different offering: human children, ewes, rams, oxen, calves, turtledoves, and, oddly enough, flour. The beast's arms were extended to receive the bodies of the children that would be placed there. The arms were constructed in such a way that they could be raised until the victim automatically rolled down to the open mouth and into the furnace so that they would be consumed by the vicious fire. The fire of the amalgamation of sacrifices burned continuously, the smoke released from the monster's nose. As this happened, the cries of the terrified children would be masked by playing of instruments, particularly the beating of drums. The word for drum was *toph,* giving the name of this ritual site: the Tophet.

Was this giant furnace an oven that baked the earliest eucharistic sacrifices and burnt offerings? Could the strange combination of ingredients burned in the seven chambers of Moloch's stomach be an antecedent to bread as a sacrificial offering? According to the Old Testament, the Lord commanded that Moses tell his people to make a burnt offering, a sacrifice in performing a vow, or in a freewill offering of what is called a "meat offering." In this offering, flour was mixed with a lamb, ram, baby goat, or young bull. When combined, the offering was to be put into a fire and offered to the Lord so that "when ye eat of the bread of the land, ye shall offer up an heave offering unto the Lord" (Numbers 15:19 KJV). Later in the New Testament, Jesus offered himself as the sacrificial lamb. The eucharistic feast consisted of the bread and wine that when consecrated, are believed to become the body and blood of Christ, thereby mixing the body and blood of the innocent sacrifice with flour, as in bread. To partake in the sacrament of Holy Communion is to partake in an alternative sacrifice to those in the days of Moloch.

The Fires of Hell

The Ammonites revered Moloch as their most important deity. Over time, as they assimilated into Arabian cultural, it is believed that the stories of Moloch inspired Arabian fire gods and eventually, the jinn. The jinn are evil beings that are represented as smoke. They are evoked by burning hair, the smoke from which they become. Historians theorize that the long-held association with demons as breathing fire or smoke and dwelling in a burning place such as Hell where the ultimate price for sin equates to torture and burning alive is linked to what happened with Moloch at the fiery Tophet. Both the Quran and the Bible imply that Satan was a fire demon, an image that persists to this day.

The association of fire with evil or Hell is rooted in sun worship. Some historians suggest that because the sun was most likely the first and most universal deity, fire was seen as the sun's earthly representative that had come down from the heavens to Earth. Therefore, if you wanted to offer something to the sun, you could just "feed" the flames of a fire. This ideology can also be seen in European folklore in which fire-worship ceremonies, Baal-fires or Bel-fires, were celebrated. In one eyewitness account, published in the *Times* in July 1871, seven bonfires were lit to celebrate the midsummer solstice. These fires were blazing at various heights around the ancient hamlet of Sound, and the local children would leap over them to symbolize passing through the fire to Moloch, "just as their ancestors would have done a thousand years ago" (Conway, 1876). Various superstitions connecting evil to fire are found throughout the ancient world.

It Burns! It Burns!

Burning huge effigies still occurs in places like the Black Rock Desert of northwest Nevada, north-northeast of Reno, at the Burning Man festival. Apart from this festival, the notion of burning a wicker man has come to signify something especially terrifying, thanks to the 1973 British horror film *The Wicker Man*. The film centers on a detective who is sent to a remote island on the Scottish coast to investigate a missing girl. I will not give away any spoilers because it is a classic film that is well worth watching. As a historian, I wholeheartedly recommend it, as it is a perfect blend of historical accuracy and creative storytelling. Not to mention, it's scary as hell!

The first mention of the Wicker Man, however, comes not from the '70s, but rather from 50 BCE in Julius Caesar's *Commentā rii dē Bellō Gallicō* (*Commentaries on the Gallic War*). In this seminal, albeit biased text, Caesar describes his observations of the religious customs of Celtic people from the nine years he spent fighting the Germans and Celts in Gaul. He writes: "Some tribes have colossal images made of wickerwork, the limbs of which they fill with living men; they are then set on fire, and the victims burnt to death" (Caesar, 2012).

Greek historian Diodorus Siculus (Diodorus of Sicily, 90–30 BCE) mentions a similar human sacrifice of the Celts, and claims they kept prisoners for up to five years in order to impale them on a stake under their diaphragms to honor the gods. Rather than burn them in a wicker man, they would simply toss all of the impaled bodies on a burning heap with a mélange of sacrificial items from the first of the harvest, like sadistic shish kebabs. Another Greek writer, known as the Great Geographer of Antiquity, Strabo mentions the use of wicker men in his text, *Geographica* (seventh century BCE). First, he tells about how the druids observed the convulsions of a newly sacrificed human to tell fortunes. He goes on to describe druidic human sacrifices during which the victim was shot with an arrow, then thrown into a huge wicker man built from straw and wood, along with cattle, wild animals, and other humans, and the whole thing burned as an offering. These are just a few examples of Celtic human sacrifices from what historians consider the most reputable sources. However, it is important to note that although the sources are good in that they are often primary accounts and textually complete, their content must always be viewed with skepticism because it could have been Roman war propaganda to use against their enemies.

Burning effigies like wicker men was a favored tradition, even when they were no longer used for human sacrifice. In Belgium, for example, huge dolls were made of woven twigs of willow or reed and simply carried in a procession. In Paris, until 1743, people would make what they called *le geant de la Rue aux Ours,* or the giant of the Rue aux Ours, one of the oldest streets in the right bank of Rouen in Paris; Rue aux Ours means "bear street." The people of Paris made this huge wicker figure dressed like a soldier, supposedly to honor the burning of a blasphemous soldier in 1418, although this is just speculation. Once they dressed the figure in regimental clothing, they paraded it up and down the streets for several days. It was finally burned on July 3 in front of a large crowd of spectators singing *Salve Regina.* A master of ceremonies presided over the ritual with a lighted torch in his hand. Pieces of the burning effigy rained down upon the people who eagerly scrambled to pick them up like kids collecting candy at an Americana Memorial Day parade.

A Germanic pagan spring tradition was to construct a doll from straw and carry it away in procession. They named the effigy Death. At the border of the village, the doll was torn apart and thrown into the water or burned as a way to ceremoniously "carry out Death." The pieces of the doll or ashes and incandescent charcoals from the incineration were taken to spread over the field. This would supposedly protect against epidemics and promote fertility. Sometimes a part of the Death doll was used to decorate a tree, or a girl was brought to the village and given the name Spring to represent her triumph over Death. The children would try to leap over the fire, a common practice in many Euro-pagan burning rituals. Again, this jumping over the fire is in reference to the "passing through the flames" required by the Baal-Bel-Moloch figure. To this day, Beltane is celebrated in some rural parts of Europe by lighting huge bonfires (the term "bonfire" came from *bone-fires*, a reference to their origins in blood sacrifice). Even in modernity, in the deepest parts of California's redwood forest, members of the Bohemian Club gather to burn an effigy, not of Death, but of *Care*, to a huge wicker man–style owl.

In midsummer, members of this elite club, including bankers, businessmen, politicians, and even presidents and prime ministers, gather in a large 2,700-acre redwood forest in Monte Rio, California. The property belongs to this very exclusive private club, whose minimum membership dues start at $25,000 and have a twenty-year wait-list. Since 1881, this has been the site of a pagan ceremony that has caused much speculation and curiosity. Deep in the forest within the Bohemian Grove lies a

160-acre grove with an artificial lake where participants hold a very rich symbolic pagan ceremony known as the Cremation of Care. The ritual is open to men only. Its stated purpose is to exorcise the devil of Care, to ensure the success of the next two weeks of their Bohemian Club meeting. The ritual is performed in front of a giant hollow statue of an owl, whom some say is meant to represent Moloch. The ritual performance is quite a spectacle with pyrotechnics, somber music, and spooky off-stage voice narration. Much like the burning of Death in the old German pagan ceremony, the burning of Care would serve as a sort of catharsis to help members triumph over there cares and ensure their good fortunes, as well as the health of the forest.

Over time, witches started to play an increasingly prominent role in such ritual burnings, and these wicker men changed into wicker witches. As the fear of witches spread, the burning of wicker witches was believed to not only provide fertility and good harvest but now also to expel evil sorcery. Occasionally, live cats were thrown into the fire and sacrificed, their ashes sprinkled in the fields to drive out mice and other vermin. Wouldn't it have been more effective to simply keep the cats around? I think they'd catch more mice alive than dead!

People struggled to understand why bad things like crop failures or livestock deaths happened in their world. As they looked for a scapegoat, it seemed that burning wicker witches was not enough. Until the time leading to the Middle Ages, the punishment for witchcraft was often limited to a fine and, at worse, banishment. Even in the Middle Ages, witchcraft was often seen as just a pagan remnant and really not too threatening. Even clergy dismissed witchcraft as just some obscure, antiquated practice that couldn't do any real harm. However, around 1430, rumors started circulating about a secret sect within Christianity—the witches. Calamities such as thunderstorms, crop failures, famine, epidemics, death, and infertility of people and cattle were increasingly blamed on old ladies. During this time, more people tried to warn against this secret sect, but their claims initially received little support. People essentially laughed them out of town and accused them as being fearful conspiracy theorists.

By the end of 1470, something had changed. Plague and famine led to the death of thousands of people and the beginning of depopulation in Europe. Against the background of this misery, people became more open to the idea of the secret witch sect. They started believing that perhaps these witches were to blame. Still, the detection and trial of these witches did not have wide support. Scholars, theologians, philosophers, and government officials did not believe that a human could perform magic. The only way that a human could perform such things would be with the help of the Devil. Therefore, witches must have made a covenant with him; they would worship him and, in return, receive great powers. Because these powers came directly from the Devil, they were evil.

Once this door was opened, everything fell into place. Now, the witches became heretics. Because they were classified as heretics, rather than superstitious old pagans, they fell under the laws that were originally founded against heretics, meaning that witches were outlaws who could be arrested and tortured in order to obtain confessions. Still, some secular and indeed some religious authorities did not believe in the witch conspiracy. Nevertheless, on December 5, 1484, Pope Innocent VIII issued a papal bull, *Summis desiderantes affectibus* (Desiring with supreme ardor), which proclaimed that unconditional support should be granted anyone fight against witches. It opened the door to witch hunts, based on the biblical verses in Deuteronomy that state:

There shall not be found among you any one that maketh
his son or his daughter to pass through the fire, or
that useth divination, or an observer of times, or an
enchanter, or a witch. Or a charmer, or a consulter with
familiar spirits, or a wizard, or a necromancer. For all
that do these things are an abomination unto the Lord:
and because of these abominations the Lord thy God
doth drive them out from before thee. (18:10–22 KJV)

Before the papal bull, the Church was historically lenient about witchcraft. In a letter to Harald III of Denmark in 1080, Pope Gregory VII said that the Church forbade the practice of executing witches for their presumed guilt of causing storms, pestilence, or crop failures. Now, with one signature, the pope unleashed a torrent of paranoia, murder, and madness. The witch hunts were about to begin, and the only way to successfully deal with witches was to burn them. To be clear, burning witches did not begin in this period, nor with the Catholic Church. It may come as a surprise, but the first references to burning witches dates back over four thousand years ago to the Sumerians. In one particular Sumerian tablet, it calls for the burning of witches, saying, "I turn to thee, I implore thee, I raise my hands to thee, I sink down at thy feet, Burn the sorcerer and the witch! Blast the life of the dreaded sorcerer and the witch" (Jastrow, 1911). There are many ancient references to burning witches, but why specifically burning?

According to the Catholic Church at the time of the witch hunts, simply hanging a witch was not enough because then the witch's soul, including the demon inside of it, could pass on to her children or any spectator at the gallows. Only fire would work, as burning was believed to be the most effective way to free their souls from the Devil. The smoke from the flames would rise up, sending their now purified souls back to their maker. In a way, they reasoned, it was the most compassionate thing to do for witches because through burning, their souls would go to heaven and they would be at peace with God and free from the Devil, who only sought to steal their souls and imprison them with him in the eternal flames of Hell.

CHAPTER 5

Early Modern Demonology

In 1567, James Charles Stuart became King James the VI of Scotland, the last of the Scottish kings, when he was just an infant. In 1603, he was also given the title King James I of England, as his predecessor Queen Elizabeth had no children. As the first king of both England and Scotland, he became the first King of Great Britain. When King James VI of Scotland officially ascended to the throne, he became known as King James VI of Scotland and King James I of England, hence the somewhat confusing title King James VI & I. In this text, he will be referred to as King James.

King James and his new bride, Anne of Denmark, set sail for Scotland. Meanwhile, on the distant shore, a coven of witches in league with the Devil himself performed a secret ritual in the hopes of causing the death of the monarch. Can witches use sorcery to bring about a ruler's death? King James was both a monarch and a witch hunter. In his lifetime, he ruled Scotland and England, wrote a detailed, scientifically ordered treatise on demonology and witchcraft, interrogated witches, and survived a malevolent attack at sea.

King James's infamous fixation with demon hunting, witches, and witchcraft is well documented throughout the historical and literary record. The witch hunts that overtook Europe between 1450 and 1750 marked a period in history when somewhere around one hundred thousand people were tried for witchcraft. By the end of this continuous fervor to stamp out witches, just under a half of those who were tried and convicted of unholy crimes were executed. Scotland's devotion to witch hunting is well known and documented, mainly through court records that have survived over the centuries. Much of the interest and concentration on the subject of witches, demons, and their practices is due to King James.

In either late August or early September 1589, following her marriage by proxy to James VI at Kronborg Castle, Anne of Denmark sailed for Scotland and her new husband. Over the next month, a succession of strange events including injuries to crew members, naval gun explosions, the death of two sailors following ships colliding within the flotilla, and perilous storms at sea cut short her trip to Scotland and ultimately forced the fleet to remain at Flicker. Anne's crews refused any further attempt to reach Scotland because it was already October. King James responded to the news of his bride nearly losing her life in the storms by amassing the royal fleet, setting sail, and coming to Anne's rescue himself. It was quite a while, however, until he could actually safely launch himself. There were continuous postponements because of the severe weather and dangerous storms at the time. On October 22, the weather cleared enough for James to embark and sail to retrieve Anne. After finally arriving, King James stayed in Denmark with Anne for six months during which time he met and debated theology with a "Danish witchcraft expert" Niels Hemmingsen in Roskilde (Stewart, 2003). The royal couple left on a return voyage that finally arrived in Scotland on the first of May in 1590. While the royal fleet sailed back to Scotland, a storm surrounded the ships. So violent were the storms on their return that the ship on which King James and Anne sailed nearly capsized and another ship was lost completely. At that same moment, it was said that on the Auld Kirk Green in North Berwick, a coven of witches and Francis Stewart, fifth Earl of Bothwell, conspired with the Devil to raise the storm in hopes of killing both the king and his bride.

Upon reaching home, King James decided that the blame would fall to witches casting evil spells upon the king, his new wife, and the royal fleet. In fact, the actions James took in response to the harrowing return voyage were unprecedented: At least seventy suspected witches were brought in from the coastal town of North Berwick to uncover the guilty party or parties. King James was certain that the storm that engulfed the fleet during the return to Scotland was produced by a conspiracy fueled by witchcraft and hatred for himself and Anne.

What is known about the plot to end the lives of King James and his bride comes from trial records of those who were tortured until they confessed their part in the assumed intrigue (Roughead, 1913). Many suspected witches were grilled and confessed, under the most severe means of torture, to a litany of grisly spells and specific ritualistic practices that were meant to bring about the king and his wife's demise at sea.

From childhood, King James had been absorbed with religion, demons and witches, and the supernatural. As a child, King James experienced the tragedy of the violent death of his mother, Mary, Queen of Scots. This may have been the event that ignited the future king's obsession with magic and the occult. Underscoring this is a ghastly story regarding the incident that

Sir John Harington wrote about in *Account of an Audience with King James I,* in Nugae Antiquae that James had told him that the queen's death "was visible in Scotland before it did really happen, being, as [King James] said, 'spoken of in secret by those whose power of sight presented to them a bloody head dancing in the air'" (Black, 2017). James was described as having been curious about witchcraft as early as 1589. Dunlap writes of this early interest noting, "When at Aberdeen [King James] insisted on seeing the 'notorious and rank' witch Marioune McIngaruch; she showed him three 'stanis' or drinking vessels used in her art" (Dunlap, 1975). Additionally, it can be assumed that the events surrounding his betrothal to Anne of Denmark must have deepened James's mounting fascination with witches and witchcraft. Like most kings, James VI was prone to a fair degree of narcissism. In James's particular case, he himself believed that due to his devotion to God and his writing skills, the Devil himself took umbrage with his very existence and therefore was out to get him in particular (Roughead, 1913).

Unlike his predecessor, Queen Elizabeth I, King James was far more extreme in his views when it came to religion. To that end, his interest in witches and witch hunting stemmed from a belief that those who engaged in witchcraft were an abomination and an effrontery to a moral society—as well as to God himself. So obsessed was the king with witches and witchcraft that, in 1597, he published a book dedicated to the subject: his *Daemonologie.* This treatise not only encouraged the practice of persecuting those individuals believed to be witches, it inspired witch hunters to greater heights in the pursuit. And because King James happened to be monarch, the book only helped to fuel the righteous indignation of those determined to end the craft and punish the accused.

The sheer popularity and frenzy of witch hunts were enormously widespread in Scotland, where it is said that as many as four thousand people, mostly women, were tortured into confessions and subsequently executed. This aggressive campaign against those who practiced witchcraft can be attributed to King James, known as the royal witch hunter.

The North Berwick Witch Trials, Daemonology, and Macbeth

Prior to 1590 public panic over witches was a rarity in Scotland although folklore about witches existed and there was a certain familiar knowledge of the subject within the populace. As the religious battle between Catholics and Protestants reared its head during the Reformation, this subject would resurface within the greater conflict. Scotland was predominantly Catholic before the Reformation. Folklore and beliefs about mystic creatures in the form of Sithean (a prehistoric burial mound in the Scottish Highlands where the fairies were believed to dwell) and witches were commonplace and part of the fabric of the country. But as the Reformation began to gain traction, Protestantism became the official religion practiced in Scotland. Folklore beliefs began to be associated by the Church of Scotland with superstition and, even worse, Catholicism. This shift also coincided with a change in potentates from Queen Mary, who was a devout Catholic, to King James, who was educated with Protestant influence. Once the dominant religion, Catholicism became associated with pagan beliefs and superstitions and was stigmatized as a result of the adoption of Protestant doctrine.

To add to the stigma, Catholicism was associated, although indirectly, with witchcraft through passage of the Witchcraft Act of 1563. As a result, it became more common for Catholicism to be linked with the idea of witchcraft. The Scottish Witchcraft Act allowed the Protestant Kirk to expose those who were deemed unreformed Catholics with the excuse that they were ridding the country of witches. The act made previously innocuous crimes of witchcraft capital offenses. Additionally, the act did not outline in detail what a witch was, so it was at the court's and accuser's discretion who was a witch and who practiced the craft. These religious strains provide the backdrop for what eventually transpired at the trials in North Berwick.

The trials in North Berwick originated with David Seaton, the local deputy bailiff of the town of Tranent. Seaton had a maidservant named Geillis Duncan. Geillis possessed the talent of curing the illnesses and injuries through rather mysterious means, which apparently troubled Seaton. To add to her boss's concern, in the middle of the night, Geillis Duncan would take walks. Things such as this would trouble the master of any house in those days, as women did not have a high degree of autonomy. Additionally, Seaton noted that Duncan's late-night wanderings seemed to be interfering with her duties around the house. At the same time, rumors were circulating around Tranent among the many healed by Geillis. Seaton came to learn from the gossip that Duncan's abilities were beyond mere natural gifts; she was performing outright miracles. The accounts he heard from those who had benefited from her gifts only deepened his suspicion. Seaton came to believe his maid had not been given divine gifts but rather had been working in concert with the Devil himself. Working himself into a paranoid lather, Seaton decided he would conduct his own interrogation of Geillis Duncan to see what she had to say about her magical gifts of healing, but the girl dodged his inquiries. At this point, David Seaton was sure Duncan was a bona fide witch, so he sought out the good people of the town to help him jail Geillis in the local tollbooth and to try her for witchcraft. Seaton and the townsfolk then acted as interrogators and proceeded to torture Geillis Duncan by using pilliwinks, which were somewhat similar to thumb screws but probably worse. Geillis's head was also bound with rope. At first, Geillis refused to confess anything, so the amateur but highly enthusiastic interrogators decided to up the ante by thoroughly searching her body to find the Devil's mark. When looking for the Devil's mark, searchers would examine the accused by stripping them. It was a humiliating ritual during which a woman's breasts, genitals, and anus could be exposed and examined because it was believed that the Devil marked them in the areas of the body that were treated with the highest degree of modesty. As one may have guessed, marks were found on her body: one on Geillis's neck and another somewhere around her genitals. At this point, she confessed that, "all her dooings [sic] done by the wicked allurements and inticements [sic] of the Dieuell, and that she did them by witchcraft" (Carmichael, 1597). When Seaton succeeded in getting the confession he had wrought out of the girl, he had Geillis thrown in prison. She remained there, where she was subjected to sustained torture for three to four months (ibid., 89).

Geillis Duncan was the first case seen in Scotland, and to that end, Seaton and his band of cohorts made things up as they went. Torture to obtain a confession was strictly illegal, but technicalities such as this were overlooked because all parties were driven by the need to obtain a confession so that the trial would reach the desired conclusion. Geillis was not executed for the crimes to which she confessed. Instead, she was allowed to remain alive because she named names during her stay in prison, most likely as a result of regular torture at the hands of her jailers. Duncan's confession established a standard for witch trials in Scotland that were carried out from that point onward. Geillis Duncan went on to accuse Agnes Sampson, Agnes Thompson, and Doctor John Fian (his alias was John Cunningham). She also named Ewphame Meealrean as the witch who cursed her god-father who had passed away, as well as Barbara Napier. Napier, Duncan claimed, cursed Archibald, Earl of Angus, with a disease that led to his death. Further prodding resulted in her confession that Robert Grierson, Janet Sandilands, and George Mott's wife were practitioners of witchcraft as well. Most of the people whom Geillis named were acquainted with each other, which strengthened suspicions and the case for them being fellow conspirators in practicing malicious and dark magic. This revelation caused Seaton and his newly deputized witch hunters to sound the alarm that they and Scotland had an outright epidemic on their hands. They subsequently hunted down the men and women whom Duncan had accused.

News of the goings-on in Tranent eventually made its way to King James. Initially, he appeared to merely be curious about the situation. The king was known for his interest in all kinds of knowledge, but several accounts indicated that the king was at least intrigued by the occult and witches. Whatever the official reason or within what capacity, he soon involved himself in the proceedings. Agnes Sampson, who was the oldest of those accused by Duncan, was summoned by King James to appear before the royal court. Sampson apparently did not please King James, and she refused to confess. King James responded by sending her back to prison, where just as Geillis Duncan had been previously, she was systematically tortured as well as forcibly examined for the Devil's mark. Initially, it appears that no mark could be discerned on her body, so the accusers moved forward and shaved off all of Agnes Sampson's body hair. In due course, after being "thrawen with a rope" a mark was discovered on her "priuities" (Carmichael, 1597). This was enough torture and humiliation for Sampson to finally admit that she was a witch, as well as backing up Duncan's assertion that the other suspects were guilty of being the same. This further captivated the king's interest in the case.

In response, he called Agnes Thompson to appear before the royal court as well. Although it is not entirely clear why, Thompson was much more forthcoming in her testimony. In fact, she confessed to being a witch as well as being in league with the Devil. Perhaps she was aware of the tactics and wished to spare herself the degradation and torture within prison. Regardless of the reason, she willingly told the king and his court a detailed account of the previous All Hallows' Eve. Thompson described a massive gathering where more than two hundred witches commenced to dance and sing while drinking wine together. It was during these festivities, Thompson alleged, that Geillis Duncan showed off a magical lute that she had used to bewitch people and control their actions. Strangely, James went as far as summoning Duncan to come and play her lute for the court. The king assured the court that they were immune to the serenading because they enjoyed the grace of God.

Although the king and the court seemed to be entertained, the fun had to end. Perhaps in hopes that the torture or imprisonment could be shortened or ended, Agnes Sampson appeared before King James in the fall of 1590 to relate tales of her cohorts in regard to witchcraft they had all practiced. The king answered Sampson's story by losing patience and accusing all of the alleged witches of lying. Agnes Sampson responded out of an apparent need to prove herself an authentic witch and did something that profoundly changed the course of the trials. Sampson requested to speak to the king directly, and when allowed, she related the pillow talk uttered by the king and queen on their wedding night. King James changed his mind entirely when he heard the words and swore to God that he believed "all the Diuels in hell could not have discouered the same" and revealed that what she had spoken to him was true (ibid., 94). Things moved quickly after this, and King James went from being intrigued and entertained to convinced and outraged. Further testimony acted only to strengthen this sentiment in the king.

As Agnes Sampson ran out of things to confess, King James called Agnes Thompson to the court in order to extract more information. Keep in mind that the torture was continuous in prison and only resulted in further revelations from the accused individuals. Thompson was no different in that she upped the ante by painting a disturbing and personally frightening confession for the king. She claimed to have attempted to poison the king with venom from a frog (ibid., 95). When the plan failed to materialize, she abandoned the idea, but not for long. She confessed that the Devil himself had pressured her to continue, the king being the very person who stood in the way. Coinciding with the king's trip to rescue Anne, Thompson brought together her fellow witches in hopes to have the king meet his end while on the high seas. For King James, this brought together the idea of witchcraft and high treason, and he viewed it as a very personal attack.

Doctor John Fian, also known as John Cunningham, the most pivotal of the accused included in Geillis Duncan's list of conspirators, was a schoolmaster from the town of Saltpans. As the only male conspirator that was accused by the former housemaid, he was said to have been the group's register and ran their meetings. Fian confessed after being tortured at length, much as the others, but not before the other conspirators had directed interrogators to search under Fian's tongue for needles said to be a charm that enabled the schoolmaster and sorcerer to resist their efforts. Fian was pivotal in his testimony because the word of a man carried much more weight; he was simply a more credible witness at this time in history. In his testimony, he confirmed previous evidence on his being a register for the group and working with the Devil. He admitted to gathering oaths from the other members and for documenting information from the Devil himself.

A stickler for the rules, his official role was to ensure that all were in attendance at their meetings and that every member of the coven adhered to those rules laid out by their master (ibid., 98). He also admitted that he drove a romantic rival to lunacy via cursing him to win the affections of a woman. The victim of this curse was summoned to appear before the court and was found to be at the very least suffering from some kind of convulsive fits (ibid., 101). Fian further pursued the woman in the story and devised a plan to have her brother steal some of her hair in order to mix up a love potion. Things went awry when the woman's mother caught her son trying to get some of his sister's hair. It turned out that the mother was a witch as well and ordered her son to take hair from a cow instead. Fian further admitted that when he used the hairs, the love spell resulted in the cow coming and attacking him instead (ibid., 102-3). Ultimately, the king believed Fian, and when the sorcerer refused to renounce the Devil, he was put to death. The other witches met similar ends because of their treason and actions against God.

A woman protests as one of her accusers, a young girl, appears to have convulsions. A small group of women were the source of accusations, testimony, and dramatic demonstrations during this early modern witch trial.

Daemonologie was published a full seven years after the North Berwick witch trials concluded in 1590. It is unknown exactly when King James began to write this treatise, but it is assumed that he was spurred on by what transpired during the trials. The common belief is that he began to write sometime after the conclusion of the North Berwick trials, then published after the end of the first group of witch trials in 1597. The king's motivation in publishing his treatise on the subject of demons and witches was to educate the public on the reality and dangers of witches. Included in the book was information on the proper procedures for prosecuting witches as well as protecting against their evil powers and practices. The king took a scientific approach to setting out a kind of rulebook for witchcraft. The book also allowed King James to paint himself as an intellectual, progressive monarch who explained things in a logical, scientific fashion. *Daemonologie* is written as a Socratic dialogue in three books/sections between Philomathes and Epistemon. The former character was the skeptic, while the latter character is written as the believer. This format lent a level of credence to the book by placing the supernatural subject matter in a scientific literary frame. King James wanted to prove that witchcraft was real and that it could be combated through a logical set of rules or steps. He also wanted to make plain that witches and witchcraft were both treason against the king and a crime against God himself. The first book attempts to divine the difference between necromancy and magic, although it categorizes both as being part of witchcraft. King James further categorizes two different forms of magic, one being malicious and the other deemed more theoretical and within the law. The second book explores harmful and malicious magic through the lens of sorcery and witchcraft and connects them to the Devil. It is in this section of the book that King James builds his definition of a standard witch. In the third book, the author covers the particulars of how to deal with witches and malicious magic as well as how to punish its practitioners, with the bottom line being to ultimately put them to death.

Shakespeare and Macbeth

Without question, the most famous literary work to draw inspiration from this period in history is Shakespeare's *Macbeth*. It is rumored that "the Scottish Play" was made short deliberately so as not to tax James's patience as he was said to loathe sitting through long productions. The king's subjects were happy to mimic his disdain for witchcraft and witches themselves. Soon after the passing of the Witchcraft Act, Marlowe's *The Tragicall History of the Life and Death of Doctor Faustus* revealed one of the most intense portrayals of witchcraft ever seen by audiences. Dramatic works have the power to influence the public's perception, and this time in Scotland was no different. Shakespeare was also to follow suit in his work.

Macbeth's inaugural performance in 1606 coincided with a visit by the queen's brother, and the king of Denmark knew firsthand of the near-death experiences of his sister and King James at sea during their journey back to Scotland. This being a state visit, the play was probably well attended. Because the drama centered around a subject so closely related to the events surrounding the king's life and interests, including of course witchcraft, it could be assumed that the king's fascination with sorcery and witches gained momentum with leading figures in the kingdom. *Macbeth* also made a connection between witchcraft and treason against the monarchy, thus underscoring what King James had been driving at with his book *Daemonologie,* and his willingness to participate in the trials at North Berwick. Additionally, the play was performed within a few months after the Gunpowder Plot, in which Guy Fawkes had attempted to blow up the king as well as Parliament on November 5, 1605.

Shakespeare interspersed the text with many references to real-life events to intensify the drama that unfolded throughout. The play's three witches, the Weird Sisters, were given authenticity through use of current events of the day. Specifically, the playwright used events surrounding the popularity of witch hunting. Being familiar with the king's authority on demonology and witchcraft, Shakespeare sought to please the ruler by emulating the black magic rituals written of in the king's *Daemonologie* to impart a realistic quality to the Weird Sisters' incantations:

> *Round about the cauldron go; In the poison'd entrails throw.*

> *Toad, that under cold stone. Days and nights hast thirty-one.*

> *Swelter'd venom sleeping got, Boil thou first i' the charmed pot.*

> *Double, double toil and trouble; Fire burn and cauldron bubble.* (Shakespeare, 1623)

It was this description in Shakespeare's *Macbeth* that gave modern popular culture our depiction of the witch—toiling over a burning cauldron, concocting strange potions with horrible ingredients. The playwright wove in another witch reference when the First Witch mentions that she set sail in a sieve, a line alluding to when one of the North Berwick witches was accused of using the same specific kind of boat. Shakespeare also cleverly referred to the king's 1589 brush with death at sea with the line (spoken by the First Witch), "Though his bark cannot be lost, Yet it shall be tempest-tost" (ibid.).

Devil Pacts

The subject of the Devil is prolific within oral tradition, as well as being found readily in any number of literary examples. Among these literary instances there lies the Devil's pact. The idea of the Devil's pact may have originated in the Old and New Testaments of the Bible, where covenants were drawn between men and God (Ball, 2014). People may have naturally assumed that if it were possible to enter into an agreement with a deity, it would be possible to draw up a contract with a malevolent force as well. History is filled with stories of Devil pacts. Because of their good versus evil dramatic themes, these stories ended up being essential sermon material for medieval priests. The earliest example of a written contract between humankind and the Devil is found in the story of Saint Theophilus of Adana. First appearing in a Greek text, then translated into Latin, Theophilus sought out a deal with the Devil in order to obtain a bishopric. Rudwin describes the events that led up to Theophilus's decision in the following passage:

> [Theophilus] was so highly esteemed by the priesthood
> and by the community that, upon the death of his bishop,
> he was considered worthy of the bishopric. But, through
> modesty, he declined the proferred dignity. The new
> bishop, to whom Theophilus was calumniated, resenting
> the fact that he was second choice, was only too glad
> to deprive him of his position in the church. In order
> to recover his post, he enlisted the services of a Jewish
> magician, who secured for him an appointment with the
> Devil. (Rudwin, 1930)

The document is signed in Theophilus's blood, but after seven years of carousing and living it up, he feels his time is growing short and thinks better of the decision. Following this change of heart, the Virgin Mary is said to have had mercy on the poor fellow. Mary goes into Hell in order to get the document back from the Devil and rescues the repentant Theophilus. This seems a somewhat trite outcome; however, the story of Theophilus is structured in a way to convince parishioners and the more common folk that it is always in their best interest to repent—in other words, keep coming to mass and the rest. One of the more famous examples of pacts with the Devil centered on Georgius Faustus. During his life, he made a living allegedly by traveling as a scholar who practiced necromancy and astrology (Ball, 2014). After his death, the real man Faustus became a legendary character in oral tradition and was the eventual inspiration for countless literary works that center on the scholarly man who desires knowledge so badly, he exchanges his soul to feed his addiction. Stories about his particular legend seem to point to knowledge and its close relative, literacy, as dangerous or even akin to the Devil.

One of the most infamous Devil's pacts is the contract between Urbain Grandier and the Devil. The pact was entered into evidence during the Loudun Possession Trial of 1634. In 1632, in the town of Loudun, in the Nouvelle-Aquitaine region in western France, a nun known simply as Sister Agnes inexplicably refused to kiss the church pyx, a small, round container used to carry the consecrated host for Holy Communion. In front of many witnesses, including the Duke of Orleans, Sister Agnes convulsed and twisted her body in unimaginable ways, bent backward until her hands touched her feet to form a circle with her spine. During this episode, she was inconsolable and uttered vulgar profanity and blasphemies that shocked everyone. She claimed it was Asmodeus who possessed her. Other Ursuline nuns in the Loudun convent had been possessed. An investigator with the Church suspected that a local priest was summoning demons.

The pact that was allegedly drawn up between Urbain Grandier and the Devil. It was entered into evidence during the Loudun Possession Trial of 1634. Signatures on the document include Astaroth, Leviathan, Satan, and other demonic entities.

A priest named Urbain Grandier was accused of multiple sexual assaults of Ursuline nuns, and he was also said to have signed a pact with the Devil. Crowds from all over Europe came to see the trial. The nuns testified that the priest Urbain Grandier was a sorcerer and that they were visited by and consequently possessed by the Devil as well. The Ursuline sisters professed to have regular fits due to their being possessed, including convulsions, ecstatic utterances, and spasms. Several years transpired where exorcisms were a common occurrence where the sisters screamed out blasphemies against God, contorted their bodies, and barked like dogs. Public panic and hysteria were the response in the area. This led to publicly performed exorcisms that regularly drew spectators. Eventually, the nuns' testimony against Grandier and several others deemed witches resulted in torture and virtually immediate confessions to whatever the inquisitors intimated in their examinations. Urbain Grandier ultimately confessed to and was convicted of sorcery and burned at the stake in August of 1634. Ironically, his own exorcists were the ones who lit the flames because, as we discussed in the previous chapter, this would be the only way to ensure the safety of others, as well as the salvation of the priest's soul. Some accounts indicated that the nuns were asked to fabricate salacious narratives in order to rid the Church of Grandier who had become a liability. The story of the Loudun possessions has been retold by both the novel *The Devils of Loudun* by Aldous Huxley and in Ken Russell's 1971 film *The Devils*. Russell's film is both disturbing and mesmerizing, like much of his work.

Demonology in the early modern era was marked by both a fear of the unknown and a profound fascination with knowledge—to know the unknown. This dual-edged sword—both attraction and repulsion—remains at the heart of the subjects within this book. Curious men such as King James endeavored to understand and control what he perceived as a threat to his monarchy and an affront to God himself by framing his personal experiences and perceptions within *Daemonologie*. But if not for his curiosity from a young age about how the Devil works through those who practice witchcraft, would that initial interest have grown into the quest he undertook throughout his adult life? The witches in the North Berwick trials may have been falsely accused of their alliance with the Devil—but one cannot ignore at the least the confession of Agnes Sampson when she spoke the very words shared between the king and queen in their bedchamber. If we are to believe the many men and women who confessed—at their peril—to the rites and ancient magic they practiced, then we must accept that they too had a sincere desire for knowledge of other natural and supernatural forces. In stark contrast to the early modern era, the next chapter uncovers practices, demons, and rites that render the curiosity and fascination explored within the early modern era trite in comparison.

CHAPTER 6

Summoning Demons

In the Mongolian countryside, a small group of government officials and researchers gather in a dimly lit hotel conference center to witness an *intentional* possession ritual. They actually hope to become possessed. A sixty-eight-year-old female shaman and her two apprentices dress in brightly colored fringed costumes. Their garb is strikingly similar to the long-fringed robes worn by the Sumerians when they worshipped their Anunnaki gods more than five thousand years ago. Depictions of such robes are found throughout the archaeological record, more recently, on a four-thousand-year-old, three-and-a-half-inch clay plaque found near the ancient city of Ur in 2013. Could such similarities be a coincidence?

As the young apprentices help the shaman armor her head in a flowered headdress covered in beads, bells, mirrors, and coins, the idle chatter in the room abruptly stops. The shaman closes her eyes and inaudibly mutters prayers to ancient spirits. The trio pick up their drums, which are adorned with swastikas.

The shrill jingle of primitive bells echoes throughout the room as the shaman dances, drums, and chants. Suddenly, an onlooker is overcome by the rhythmic drumming and incantations. He leaps into the arms of onlookers who restrain him. The dancers crowd around him and continue to beat their drums and shout. The shaman appears agitated; she shakes and breathes hard. Did the ritual work? Did an entity take over the body of the onlooker?

As if startled from a sleep, a government official looks up, his eyes transfixed on the shaman. He never breaks his stare and appears oddly mesmerized by the whole thing. Perhaps he is hopeful that the shaman he has called upon has delivered on her promise. You see, this ritual was not undertaken to heal, like so many shamanistic rituals. Instead, the goal of this ceremony was to summon an otherworldly entity and ask for its help. The entity was invoked to restore the harmony that was lost to this Mongolian village because of heavy rains and flooding (sometimes multiple entities are petitioned). Was this government official pleased? Perhaps instead he was fearful—fearful of what he had just helped to unleash.

The shaman gets up and spins with increasing speed as her fabric fringe whirls around. The others join, spinning in rhythmic synchrony, like Technicolor Sufi dervishes. As they spin, the dancers' ancient costumes lightly graze the tops of their Chuck Taylor sneakers, a jolting reminder that this ancient rite of possession is in fact happening to modern people in a modern era.

As a Westerner, I harbor my own intrinsic bias. I can't help but focus on the swastikas with a sense of slight discomfort, even though I fully understand that on the Indian subcontinent and in many other parts of Asia, what Westerners see as Nazi symbolism, they still recognize as a sacred symbol of Buddhism, Hinduism, and Jainism. In the archaeological record, the swastika is found through many ancient civilizations, as far-reaching as the Indus Valley and Mesopotamia. It was not until the 1930s that this spiritual mark became the emblem of evil, when the Nazi party adopted it as their own. The West still stigmatizes this holy symbol, associating with the antithesis of our values. To see it used in a ritual meant to summon demons adds to the element of fear and discomfort. However, this ancient rite has roots far deeper than even the swastika.

The question of demonic possession is as old as civilization itself. Since ancient times, most cultures have believed in the existence of spirits, and likewise, that these spirits can enter and control a person. The earliest exorcists were shamans, a fact we will examine fully in the next chapter. These shamans believed in many magical and supernatural forces and routinely performed healing rituals on people to expel demons. Yet, in the case of the Mongolian possession ritual, the shaman's aim was not to exorcise a spirit, but to summon a spirit to enter a human. This may at first seem in conflict with what we know about shamanistic healing practices, but conjuring demons to help in mankind's problems is also an ancient tradition, and one with a surprising connection to one of the most powerful rulers in human history—King Solomon.

Solomon's Magic Ring

Legend has it that King Solomon had a magical signet ring that could conjure demons. The ring was made from iron, brass, and four jewels. The image engraved on the ring was the Seal of Solomon, a hexagram composed of two intertwined triangles, situated inside a circle. In some medieval Jewish, Islamic, and Christian texts, the ring is said to have had "the Greatest Name of God" on it that remained hidden and unknown to anyone else. The story of how Solomon acquired this talisman is told in the Testament of Solomon, a mysterious text that claims to be the words of King Solomon himself. Scholars disagree over the true origins of this text. Some believe it was written between the first and fifth centuries CE by a Christian writer from Greece. Others contend that although it may have been written between the first and fifth centuries CE, it was copied by Jewish scribes in the Library of Alexandria from a much older original document. Although its origins are sketchy, the text opens with a firm declaration that this is indeed the testament of King Solomon, son of David, who reigned in Jerusalem and harnessed the power of demons to build his magnificent temple—the temple that housed the Ark of the Covenant.

During the construction of King Solomon's Temple, the son of one of his master craftsmen came to the site to help his father work. Solomon felt a deep affection for the boy, as did all the other builders. He even gave the boy double wages and a double supply of food. Over time, Solomon noticed the boy was pale, thin, and sickly. He asked the boy why he looked so ill: "Do I not love thee more than all the artisans who are working in the Temple of God? Do I not give thee double wages and a double supply of food? How is it that day by day and hour by hour thou growest thinner?" (McCown, 1915). The boy explained that every night, a demon appeared in his room and took his food, then sucked the blood from the boy's right finger and took what was left of his energy.

This troubled Solomon, so he prayed to God, and the archangel Michael appeared before him. In his hand he had a ring that bore a hexagram within a circle. "Take, O Solomon, king, son of David, the gift which the Lord God has sent thee, the highest Sabaoth. With it thou shalt lock up all demons of the earth, male and female; and with their help thou shalt build up Jerusalem" (ibid.).

From King Solomon's grimoire. Solomon seals or key, from King Solomon's grimoire

Solomon gave the ring to the boy and explained to him how he could use it for protection against this demon visitor. That night, the demon came to the boy once again, but this time, the boy threw the ring at the chest of the demon and shouted, "In the name of God, King Solomon calls thee hither!" as instructed by Solomon. Then, the demon was bound in chains. The demon panicked and promised the boy all the gold on Earth if he would let him go, but the boy did not. Instead, he took his demon prisoner back to King Solomon. Solomon demanded to know the demon's name. After some reluctant banter, the demon claimed his name was Ornias and that he resides under the star sign Aquarius in the night sky. The relationship between the demons and the stars is a strange and interesting consistency in the Testament of Solomon. Each demon reigns over a particular zodiacal sign. Some of the more interesting demons helping build the temple were the Seven Star Sisters, which is understood to be a reference to the Pleiades. These spirits were bound together, speaking all together but with one voice, saying, "We are of the thirty-three elements of the cosmic ruler of the darkness" (ibid., 34). Solomon then seals the demon with his magic ring and demands him to go to work building his temple. The demon Ornias offers Solomon a deal. He says he will call up his fellow demons to help build his temple, so long as Solomon gives him some bit of freedom, as the entity hated chains. Solomon agrees, but called upon the archangel Uriel to guard Ornias. He then gives the demon his magic ring and instructs him to use it to capture his brethren and summon them hither. Ornias amasses a crew of horrendous demons to help complete the temple.

Of all the entities that helped build King Solomon's Temple, one was especially wretched and wielded great influence over humankind—Asmodeus. Asmodeus was considered the demon of occult wisdom and human technological advances. He is the successor to the Egyptian god of wisdom and learning, Thoth, both of whom are linked to the star Sirius. In Islamic tradition, Asmodeus is a jinn, the same jinn that cheated Aladdin out of his ring to secure the magic lamp. In Jewish mysticism, according to the Zoharistic Kabbalah, Asmodeus was the love child of King David and the queen of demons, a succubus named Agrat Bat Mahlat. In Eastern European Jewish culture, Asmodeus is described as a *shed,* or evil spirit, that came from the union of a fallen angel and the sister of Tubal-Cain.

A Promethean figure, Asmodeus was revered during the Renaissance; great thinkers and humanists such as Giovanni Boccaccio claimed that they channeled this demon while writing their great works. The demon's origin and attributes are remarkably similar to Lucifer's, in that he had fallen from grace and give inspiration and education to the ignorant humans on Earth. More powerful than even Beelzebub, Pope Gregory the Great declared that Asmodeus was a supreme angel of the Order of Thrones, a commanding Christian hierarchy of angels. During the Crusades, Pope Gregory the IX claimed there were secret groups worshipping Asmodeus throughout northern Europe and in 1232 began a Crusade against the Stedingers, a group of Germanic peasant farmers who themselves were Roman Catholic. The pope accused these peasants of worshipping Asmodeus and performing unspeakable acts against their local priests, including nailing priests to the wall with arms and legs spread out to mock and deride the crucifixion of Christ.

Asmodeus was believed to have wreaked havoc in Europe. Remember, it was Asmodeus, as previously discussed, who was believed responsible for possessing Sister Agnes of Loudun in 1635 after Urbain Grandier signed his Devil's pact. Vestiges of Asmodeus are still found throughout Europe, like the inexplicable statue of Asmodeus in the Church of Saint Mary Magdalene in Rennes-le-Château, the place made famous by Baigent, Leigh, and Lincoln's *The Holy Blood and the Holy Grail* (1982), and more recently, Dan Brown's *The Da Vinci Code*, published in 2003. Some believe that the statue represents Asmodeus guarding King Solomon's Temple, as the floor beneath him resembles the "Mosaic Pavement" of the ground floor of King Solomon's Temple, described by thirty-third degree mason Albert Pike (Pike, 1900). Others believe that the statue looks down on the black-and-white-tiled floor as if observing a symbolic chess game between earthly kings, laughing at their futility, as he knows he holds the true dominion over all the material world.

Asmodeus in the Church of Saint Mary Magdalene
in Rennes-le-Château.

For the 3.6 billion people of Abrahamic faiths, it may come as a surprise that their much-revered King Solomon was associated with demonic collusion and possession. It would not, however, come as a surprise to those familiar with the occult or initiates of mystery schools such as Freemasonry. As mentioned, Asmodeus was the offspring of a fallen angel and the sister of Tubal-Cain. The very name of Tubal-Cain is the secret password of a Master Mason, as well as type of a Masonic handshake. This is no coincidence. The story of constructing Solomon's Temple, demons and all, is an essential part of Masonic tradition.

Masonic Demon Worship?

According to the tradition of Speculative Masonry (the type of Masonry that works in the philosophical realm rather than in actual stonework), the goal of its members is to create a sort of utopia for all who joined the Brotherhood. This is what they call "the Great Work," which will supposedly result in the building of a new Solomon's Temple. This is not a temple in the material sense, however. According to thirty-third-degree Freemason and Master Rosicrucian Manly P. Hall, this new perfected temple will be "the perfected temple of the human body, the perfected temple of the universe and the perfected temple of the soul" (Hall, 1934). Hall goes on to reveal that the true Temple of Solomon is "slowly being rebuilt in man as the temple of the Soul of Man" (ibid., 81). If Solomon's Temple is to be rebuilt in man as a spiritual temple of the soul, rather than a physical building, then are demonic spirits still an essential part of the construction process? Do Masons summon demonic entities to help them with their "Great Work"? Throughout history, many have believed this to be the case, which has led to fear and even hatred of Freemasonry. We've seen that it is not unusual for people in ancient history and even modernity to try to initiate their own possession or call upon demons for help, so could these conspiracies hold any truth?

In 1896, Arthur Edward Waite, occultist, renegade scholar, and cocreator of the popular Rider-Waite Tarot deck, published his book *Devil-worship in France: Or, the Question of Lucifer; a Record of Things Seen and Heard in the Secret Societies According to the Evidence of Initiates.* In this book, Waite describes the initiation ritual of the Palladian Rite of Freemasonry, the very top of the hierarchy of Masonic rites, organized and led by Albert Pike. Pike taught that divinity is of dual nature and that Lucifer is equal to God in terms of power (Starr Miller Paget, 1933). Pike also taught that it is Lucifer worshipped within this Rite of Freemasonry (ibid.). In the Palladian Rite, the term Palladian comes from *Pallas,* which refers to the Greek figure Pallas, son of the first werewolf, Lycaon, and the teacher of Athena, goddess of wisdom and war.

In 1880, while working as a physician on the steamboat *Anadyr,* Dr. Bataille met a dying Italian silk merchant named Gaëtano Carbuccia. Carbuccia told Dr. Bataille about the demonic rituals of the Palladian Rite of Freemasonry. This piqued Dr. Bataille's interest, and he soon went on a global expedition to infiltrate and observe these rituals. His testimonies were published about a decade later. So, what happened behind the closed doors of the Palladian Lodges?

During one ritual, secret society initiates worshipped at an altar to Baphomet that was adorned with three skulls of Masonic martyrs, including that of Jacques de Molay. As they worshipped, it was said that Lucifer appeared as a shining figure in physical form. Another account places the doctor during a similar ritual in Sri Lanka, where he saw woman who looked dead, or at least close to it. Out of nowhere, the woman got up and crawled over to an altar under a Baphomet statue, before being burned alive by the Brothers of the Lodge, as they chanted demonic evocations.

In a French colonial settlement in India, Dr. Bataille found one of the most gruesome sights he had yet seen or, perhaps worse, smelled. He recounts, "the ill-ventilated place reeked with horrible putrescence" (Waite and Gilbert, 2003). The Lodge members had been gathered around another Baphomet statue for so long, they were wasting away, their bodies rotting from infected skin ulcers. Others had rats biting their faces and stunk of gangrene like barely sentient corpses. Dr. Bataille describes a disturbing scene wherein the eyeball of one of the initiates hung out of its socket and dangled beside the man's cheek. Every time he tried to open his mouth to invoke the name of Beelzebub, his flaccid eyeball would roll into his mouth and muffle his speech.

When these invocations failed to conjure a demon, they would bring out a woman and burn her at the altar. Still no demon appeared, so Lodge members brought out a white goat. The Grand Master set the goat upon the alter of Baphomet and tortured it. The goat was then set on fire and cut open so that its entrails could be spread on the steps. All the while, the initiates uttered abominable blasphemies against God. When this still did not work, they resorted to slicing the throat of one of the half-dead worshippers. At last, no demon appeared. The doctor continued his ethnographical study of Palladium Freemasons, witnessing numerous animal sacrifices, human levitation, and necrophilia. On one occasion, he witnessed the demon Asmodeus materialize in a Lodge and eventually claim a human woman as his bride.

Baphomet.

On April 19, 1897, at a conference held at the Hall of the Geographic Society in Paris, a man named Marie Joseph Gabriel Antoine Jogand-Pagès, writing under the pen name Léo Taxil, stepped forward and publicly announced that he was, in fact, the creator of the testimonies of Dr. Bataille. He claimed it had all been a hoax to mock Christianity's view of Freemasonry.

With nothing but historical accounts, faulty recollections, and even the occasional hoax, it seems nearly impossible to prove or disprove historical accounts of demonic possession. What about now, though? In our postmodern society, armed with science and technology, how can we investigate the possibility of demonic possession, or should we? The Vatican seems to think there is still a need. In fact, they claim the need for exorcists is on the rise.

Possession Pandemic

Pope Francis has sanctioned a group of 250 priests spread across thirty countries who are trained to perform exorcisms. They are formally recognized as the International Association of Exorcists. Reverend Francesco Bamonte, head of the association, announced that this was good news because "exorcism is a form of charity that benefits those who suffer" (French, 2014). Granting legal recognition to this group is quite extraordinary. In a modern world with a pope who is trying to be progressive, endorsing the idea of possession and demonic entities is quite shocking. Maybe this news speaks more to the state of the Catholic Church, rather than the state of exorcism, in general. Although in the past, the Church was the first place you would look to find help with possession, now it may be the last resort, having taken a backseat to psychology and psychiatry.

Now, doctors know of quite a few disorders that were once blamed on demonic possession. Epilepsy is often a cause of the symptoms of demonic possession, as are Tourette's syndrome and schizophrenia. Evidence proving demonic possession is elusive, at best, although in the Islamic world, scientific research into demonic, or jinn, possession is currently underway, which we will examine further in chapter 11.

The current thought is that jinn can be the cause of the psychological disorder, thereby recognizing modern diseases while still allowing for the possibility of demonic possession. According to some Muslim scholars, evil jinn can invade the part of the human brain responsible for the regulation of the neurotransmitters. The jinn does not enter the brain itself, but its presence in the bloodstream is enough to affect the hormones and neurotransmitters of a person, thereby altering their mood and behavior. Some Muslim researchers have suggested that the presence of jinn can be detected by an MRI (magnetic resonance imaging). The presence of jinn in the human brain can cause psychical as well as emotional trauma. The jinn patiently waits for the perfect moment to manifest violently so it can inflict the most physical and mental damage to the possessed. However, the jinn does not always create symptoms in its victim. Instead, a victim can experience periods of ups and downs. The jinn is always present in the brain of the possessed and only manifests on specific occasions. A person exhibiting psychological problems will often have trouble in many areas of life. They can hit rock bottom, turn to drugs and alcohol, and fall into the deepest depths of depression, even becoming suicidal. This is the mission of a jinn: to destroy a person in body, mind, and spirit.

It is true that in developing countries, there is a higher rate of belief that demons are to blame for man's ills. For instance, studies in Nigeria and Cameroon have reported that 86 percent of people who suffer from epilepsy believe it to be a sign of demonic possession or bewitchment (Osungbade and Siyanbade, 2011). Yet, in contemporary Western culture, the belief in demonic possession is much less common. The similarity is that those with less education seem to have an easier time believing in the existence of a "devil." Extrapolating from the results of NORC's *General Social Survey* at the University of Chicago, 45 percent of American adults believe that the Devil probably exists. However, those with four or more years of college are less likely to believe than those with less education. Belief in the Devil decreases with social class: 73 percent of the lower class, 71 percent of the working class, 60 percent of the middle class, and 32 percent of upper class are believers (Davis, Smith, and Marsden, 2006). It seems pretty cut and dry; wealthy, educated adults in the developed world are the least likely to believe in the devil, let alone demonic possession. So how do you explain the account of Paula, a successful businesswoman with an advanced degree in chemistry from UCLA, who claims to have been possessed by the demon Haagenti for nearly a decade?

Paula's Account

In early December of 2015, I received an email from a woman who said she heard me interviewed on *Coast to Coast AM* a couple months earlier. Although I had not discussed demons on the show, she expressed to me that she felt that I might be someone who could listen to her without judgment, and that she'd been experiencing something traumatic and otherworldly. Her experiences weren't directly related to the topics of the radio show or the book I was promoting. They were about her personal account of what she felt was a demonic possession.

I let her know that I had been planning this book since 2014 and had been researching what evil meant to different cultures throughout history. The concept of the book was still in the very preliminary stages, but I mentioned to her that I was considering discussing the subject of possession. I went on to tell her that I was certainly no expert in these areas and really wouldn't be some-one who could offer anything more than a sympathetic ear with regard to her ordeal. Without knowing anything more about what she had experienced, I told her that if she wanted to share her account with me, I could, with her permission, consider includ-ing an anonymous version of it in my book if or when I moved forward with *Evil Archaeology*. She agreed, as long as I only used her first name and promised not to reveal her true identity, so we agreed to call her "Paula." Paula hopes that by sharing her story, others will have a better understanding of what people in her situation go through. This is her story.

Dear Dr. Lynn,

Thank you again for being there. I'm sorry that I took so long to get this to you. This isn't the kind of thing that someone usually talks about, and I wasn't sure where to begin, or if I even should. I think that if I ever told anybody else, they'd lock me away and think I was totally crazy. What happened to me happened back in the '90s, and I've got a new family now and I've just never gotten this off my chest. I don't think I'll ever be able to tell this to anyone else, not even my husband, so I'm grateful for this opportunity.

I've lived in the suburbs of Sacramento, California, my entire life. I was lucky enough to grow up with both my mom and dad. I was an only child, but I didn't mind. We had a pretty nice house, and I had a great group of friends. We spent a lot of time at Sunrise Mall or getting rides from my best friend Jen's mom down to Tower Records. It was a great time to be a teenager.

I went to UC Davis to study business, and then I stayed on for my MBA. I lived on campus for my first three years and I was actively involved with Greek life. I graduated in '98, and I've worked for a couple of large employers in Sacramento up until recently. I was planning on moving to the Bay Area at some point after graduation, but I don't really think I ever wanted to leave Sacramento, especially since my dad died.

My dad was a regional salesman for an aerospace technology company at the time. I loved my dad so much, but he was gone a lot when I was a kid, usually in Seattle. I'll never forget my mom calling me in 2008 to tell me that he was missing. It's one of those times, like when Kennedy was shot or 9/11. You just remember every little detail like it was in slow motion. It was about 11:00 in the morning on a Wednesday in April. My mom called me at work, which she never did, and told me that my dad's car was found abandoned next to a cliff along the PCH in Sonoma County, and that he hadn't been heard from by his job since the previous week. I was so stunned that I couldn't utter a sound, partly from shock and from a strange sense of guilt. This was probably the first sign that I had something crazy happening with me because I somehow knew that he died, and I knew how he died.

I had been having weird dreams about my dad's death before it happened. Nightmares, really, like I killed him. I was having these nightmares for days before my mom called me, then I had some kind of déjà vu experience while I was in my office the Friday before I found out my dad was gone. I could "see" my dad falling off a cliff and hitting the rocks, then big waves crashing on the rocks, and he was washed away. This was very scary, and I felt like I was on the verge of a mental breakdown when my mom told me about the car because I knew right where it was. Was I psychic or something?

At the time, I was engaged to a guy I met at work. He was very ambitious. He had big plans after receiving his MBA at Stanford to make VP within five years at his company, and then eventually, he wanted to start a private wealth management firm. I really liked his drive and ambition, and I thought I could see myself settling down with him. We dated for about two years before he proposed; his parents sent us to Hawaii where he popped the question. I said yes, and we started planning an amazing wedding. His mom started to take over all the wedding planning, and it reached a point I couldn't even take it. She acted like she was the one getting married, and she really got under my skin. His parents were taking care of everything—the wedding, the reception, the best gifts, the guest tabs, and our honeymoon—so I didn't think I should rock the boat by complaining about my future mother-in-law to my fiancé right before they give us a dream wedding. Still, it felt as though something was always bubbling underneath the surface.

A few weeks before the wedding, my friends threw me a bachelorette party. We all went out, had a lot of fun, and came back to a friend's apartment to watch movies and basically have an old-fashioned girl's night like when we were teenagers. At about 3:00 a.m. one of my friends lit candles and incense and turned off the lights. Then she got out a Ouija board. I had never even seen one before, so I was a little spooked but intrigued at the same time. She asked me if I'd ever been part of a séance before. I told her that I hadn't, and she said that we'd be able to ask the spirit world about dead people and that we could conjure ghosts. I almost started to cry because I was still pretty drunk, and I thought that I might be able to talk to my dad.

We all sat around the kitchen table, and I watched while others put their hands on the little pointer and started asking questions. I wasn't sure I believed that anything supernatural was happening because I think I expected weird magic to happen, like the pointer to move on its own. Later, people changed seats and my friend wanted me to try, so I sat at the table and put my hands on the pointer. Another girl was sitting on a stool with a pad, and she wrote down whatever the board spelled. I wasn't sure what to ask, so I just went ahead and asked if my dad was there. The pointer went into a bunch of figure eights, and then it spelled out "YES." Someone else asked something like, "If this is Paula's dad, prove it. How did you die?" I never really told anyone about how my dad died, except for my best friend Jen because we were friends since we were kids. I was very freaked out when the pointer went into a bunch more figure eights, then spelled "FALL." No one in that room could've known that! I needed to know more, so I asked what my mom's name was and it spelled it out. Again, no one knew that, and at that point I was so afraid that I just wanted to stop. I pulled my hands away from the pointer, and right as I did that, it felt like I got hit in the chest with something hard that knocked the wind out of me, and I fell backward out of the chair.

Everyone screamed, and all the candles suddenly went out. My friend lit a cigarette lighter, and I could have sworn that I saw a large, black, shadow-like figure in the corner of the room. He looked like he was wearing a hat. I screamed again until somebody flipped on the lights, and there was nothing there. With the lights on, people started to chuckle and act like that was great, but I was really disturbed and just wanted to go back home. The girl who lived there had a cat, and it came into the kitchen and stared into the corner where I thought I saw the figure moments before. It growled, then it put its ears back and hissed, then ran away, and we left right after that.

About five months after I got married, I went to my husband's parents' lake house for Thanksgiving. I don't really cook, so I didn't bring anything, but his mom was drinking wine all day, and she was starting to run her mouth. I walked into the kitchen later while the guys were watching football, and I overheard my husband's mom complaining to my sister-in-law about me not bringing a dish to dinner. I just felt a sense of rage, and I looked at the counter where a group of empty glasses were waiting to go into the dishwasher. I believe that I somehow made them all fly off the counter and get smashed into pieces against the island.

We stayed over that night because the drive back from Lake Shasta was a long one. We went to bed late, and when the house was quiet and dark, I woke up and I thought for sure that I saw a large, dark figure standing at the foot of the bed. It looked like a living shadow, and I wasn't sure if I was even awake, but I looked over at my husband who was sleeping deeply, then back at the figure. It walked over to the bedroom door and opened it, then motioned me out. I felt compelled to follow it, even though I was terrified.

What happened next felt like a bad dream. I walked, but it felt like I was floating. I found myself in the kitchen near the sink when my mother-in-law's annoying Lhasa Apso ran in, and barked and growled at me. She was trying to bite my leg when my mother-in-law came in, flipped on the lights, and asked me what I was doing out in the house without any clothes on. She picked up her dog and went back to bed, saying terrible things about me being indecent as though I couldn't hear her. I was incensed that the dog actually bit me, and I got back into bed seething with anger. My head started pounding behind my eyes, and I was having a hard time breathing, and I could somehow "see" the dog, walking around in circles and panting on my mother-in-law's bed. In my mind, I felt like I started crushing the dog's neck with my hand. I remember crying because I didn't want to do any of those things and it felt like I wasn't in control.

The next thing I knew, my husband was nudging me to wake up. It was 11:30 in the morning. I could see the lake through the pine trees from our window, but the light hurt my eyes. I felt hung over. My husband told me that his mom's dog died in the night and she wanted to know if I gave the dog table scraps from the Thanksgiving dinner the day before. His mom was beside herself because the dog was only four. I thought, of course I was being blamed.

We were invited back to the lake house for Christmas, which was the last thing I wanted to do. I was becoming an angry person and snapped at my husband more frequently. I was unpleasant at work and I actually verbally abused a client over the phone, which led to me getting corrective counseling through HR. I never got into trouble for anything before. I didn't know what was happening, and I didn't know what, if anything, I could do about it. All of this drove a wedge between us. So much that I ended up moving out.

I went to my mom's house to talk about the troubles I had been having and ask her what to do about my marriage. I had brought a big salad over for dinner. I was having so many conflicting feelings and strange dreams that I was beginning to think I was losing grip on reality. I thought that I was too young for a mental breakdown, and I wanted to know from my mom if any type of mental illness ran in our family. Shortly after I got there, she told me that she had decided to sell the house. My aunt in Michigan had an in-law suite at her house, and she offered it to my mom as a way to get away from the pain of losing my dad and her mom one after the other. This was my mom's younger sister, and she was a teacher at a high-end private school near Birmingham, Michigan. Her husband was an executive at GE in Detroit, so they had plenty of money, but I was just livid at this news, and I threw the dinner that I brought all over the floor and screamed obscenities at my poor mother. I stomped on the food and made a terrible mess, and then I urinated on the mess I made. My mom was stunned. Rather than embarrassment, I just felt enraged, so I stormed out. I immediately went to stay with my best friend, Jen.

I slept for hours and didn't wake up until sometime in the middle of the next night. My room was dark, and it felt like my husband was in the room, rolling me onto my stomach. I was still kind of groggy and my chest was very sore, but I tried to push myself up and turn over and all of a sudden, I was forced back down. I felt weight and pressure behind me, but no warmth. It was actually very cold, and I was unable to move. After that, I could hear a deep and frightening voice, in my head, but it wasn't making any sense. I heard words, but they weren't English. I tried to scream, but I was unable to move or make a sound. I wasn't sure if I was dreaming this or if someone was in my room, but I felt like I was being assaulted. I was never more afraid in my life!

After this event, I felt like I was stuck in some kind of nightmare. All I could hear were moans and screaming and I was freezing. That's all I can remember, but Jen told me that she waited until the following afternoon to check on me because I was still sleeping and she knew I was going to be late for work. She said she opened my door and almost puked because the smell in the room was so bad. She said I was in bed shivering so hard that it looked and sounded like the bed was vibrating.

She came over to try to wake me up by shaking my shoulder, and she said that I opened my eyes and grabbed her wrist and squeezed it so hard that she thought I broke it. She said that she heard a deep man's voice saying something crazy, but it was me. I don't remember any of this, and I still feel terrible about it!

Jen didn't know what to do. She said that she tried to clean me up and cover me and a few people showed up later with the woman who had the Ouija board. That woman claimed that she was a clairvoyant and that she thought I was possessed by something that I conjured up at her house, possibly a demon. Jen wasn't into the supernatural stuff, and she wasn't buying any of it. She thought this woman was a crackhead and was about to tell her to leave when I apparently sat straight up, looked right at the woman, and told her that she would die soon of the same cancer that her older sister died from, and then I laughed and fell back down. I didn't know this woman and had no idea she had a sister who died.

Jen was also like me in that she didn't go to church. She wasn't necessarily an atheist; we just didn't really think about God. She was very scared, and she believed that I was very mentally ill or possibly possessed. She told me that she thought the best thing to do was to rule out the possessed part because I didn't have health insurance or family who could pay for treatment in a mental health hospital, but she could go talk to a priest for free. Her entire knowledge of possession came from movies, so even though she'd only been in a Catholic church once or twice for a wedding, she locked me in the apartment and went to the closest church.

She said that when a twenty-year-old girl goes into a Catholic church and tries to tell a priest that her friend may be possessed, it's not easy to be taken seriously. She said that she met with a priest and tried to tell him what happened with me, but that the priest was kind of smiling, then asked her some routine questions about her home life, drugs, and so on. He never took her seriously, so she left and went to the library to look up other Catholic churches in the phone book (we didn't have the Internet then). She said she found a church in Sacramento that had Spanish mass and that she thought she might have better luck asking for help there. She found a Mexican priest who also spoke English to follow her to our apartment.

Jen said that when she opened the door, I was standing on the couch with my eyes closed and my arms straight out to my sides. She said that I walked like a zombie and crawled into bed, and then the priest started to pray, and I sat up and yelled terrible things at the priest in a deep Spanish voice, but I don't know Spanish. The priest told her that I said his mother's name and called her things like "whore," and then I fell back down and was asleep again.

She said that after that, the priest had her go through both of our closets and get every belt and purse strap that we had, and then he used them to strap my arms to the bed frame, so I couldn't get up anymore. He left after that and came back the following afternoon with another priest and some books. Jen told me that they were praying in Spanish, English, and Latin and that they were burning holy smoke and holding their crosses with the beads, but I just kept sleeping. She said that the second priest tried to open my mouth to put a wafer in and that I had puked across the room when it touched my mouth. She said that I broke out of about three or four belts with my right arm and was swinging at everyone and going crazy with my legs. She said that after that, I was screaming, then growling, then cursing in Spanish. She told me that one of the priests tried to strap my loose arm back down and that I grabbed him by his belt buckle and picked him up off his feet and threw him down to the floor. She was so afraid that the priests would leave, but they didn't.

Jen said that the priests came and went over the course of the next four or five days. They tried to feed me some kind of liquid food from Jen's drugstore and sometimes I would eat, and sometimes I would spit it at them. She said that there were times when my whole bed would shake and there would be noises in other parts of our apartment, like banging and thumps or scratching sounds. She said that whenever the priests tried to make me have communion wafers or if they sprinkled me with holy water that I'd act like a wild animal. The priests asked Jen if she knew if I was baptized and when she told them I wasn't, they got ready to perform a baptism, and that's when the scariest things happened. I was told that I went from being very violent to being very calm, but my blanket that was covering me moved off of me slowly, on its own, like it was crawling by itself. Jen said that I began to sing in some kind of weird falsetto, then cried like a little girl while I was laying there opening and closing my legs. She said that the priests jumped back when this strange symbol that looked kind of like an upside down 7 combined with part of an "S" showed up on my stomach, like it was scratched in. They went ahead with the baptism and apparently when the priest sprinkled the holy water on my head, it turned to steam as if my forehead was on fire and my eyes rolled back in my head, then I just stopped moving and went limp. I don't remember any of these things. I only know from what others tell me. I have a little awareness or familiarity when I am told about it, like I was there, but not. Maybe more like I was having an out of body thing happen. It's hard to explain.

I woke up some time after this. I had this dream where I was in total darkness, but then the darkness turned into a giant bat-like thing and flew away and there was white light everywhere. When I was finally awake, I was very confused and scared because the last thing I remembered was that I felt like I was being assaulted. I felt like I was hit by a truck. Everything smelled awful and then I saw Jen crying next to me. I took the longest shower of my life later and ended up throwing away my bed and blankets.

I cannot tell you that I know exactly what happened, but this was my experience. I never saw the priests again, and I ended up losing Jen. I loved her so much, and I still do, but sometimes people go through things that they can't comprehend or ever talk about. This event lasted about seven days altogether, and it was probably harder on her than it was on me in the long run. Our relationship was never the same after this, and we just drifted apart. I only hope that somewhere out there, she'll have an opportunity to read this, and she can know that I'm forever in her debt, and she'll always be in my heart. Thank you again for listening and letting me get this out.

While this was my rock bottom, I am happy to say that things are much better now. My husband and I got back together. He encouraged me to seek counseling, and we started attending church together. In some ways, it almost brought us closer as a family because if we can get through that (whatever that was) we can get through anything. We even renewed our vows last year at our church. I pray a prayer of thanks and deliverance to God every day.

CHAPTER 7

What an Excellent
Day for an Exorcism

Through his profanity-laden rant, Ronnie struggled to break free from the clutches of the hulking red demon. Smaller, more menacing demons danced around his feet as he struggled to not slip on their glistening trails of slime. The demon tried to force him nearly two thousand feet down into a fiery pit. During his struggle, deep scratches appeared on his limp body; one spelled "Hell," and the other resembled a figure with webbed wings like a bat. In all capitalized letters, the word *EXIT* etched itself on the boy's chest. Maybe Ronnie should never have played with that Ouija board.

Months ago, Ronnie's aunt, described as a spiritualist, came for a visit and brought with her a Ouija board. Little did she know this would be the beginning of a nightmarish experience for her nephew. She would never find out either, as she died shortly after her visit. The death of his favorite aunt was perhaps more than the Ronnie could handle. Or maybe he suffered from undiagnosed temporal lobe epilepsy, which is known to cause violent convulsions and a fixation on religious or philosophical ideas, as well as religious hallucinations (Dewhurst and Beard, 1970). As previously discussed, epilepsy is still mistaken for demonic possession in some cultures today. We may never know for sure, but on Friday, August 20, 1949, the *Washington Post* published Ronnie's story in what they dubbed "one of the most remarkable experiences of its kind in recent religious history" (Brinkley, 1949). This fourteen-year-old boy was possessed by a demon that even his Evangelical Lutheran pastor couldn't expel. After counseling the boy's parents, the pastor told them they need the help of a Catholic priest. During a marathon exorcism by the Catholics, it was reported by a Protestant minister that he personally witnessed that a "heavy armchair in which the boy was sitting with his knees drawn under his chin tilted slowly to one side and fell over, throwing the boy on the floor" (ibid.).

Ronnie's account was the real-life story behind the 1971 novel *The Exorcist*. The details were changed from a fourteen-year-old boy to a thirteen-year-old girl in order to protect the boy's identity. The book inspired a film by the same name, directed by William Friedkin. A number of people who worked on the production claimed that the movie itself was cursed. Even William Peter Blatty, author of the original book, said that strange things happened during the making of the film, including a studio fire that destroyed all the interior sets of the house, except for the bedroom of the main character, Regan (Burstyn, 2006). Additionally, Linda Blair, who played Regan, had her back broken during an exorcism scene. Burstyn, who played Regan's mother, also broke her back during filming. It got so bad on the set, that the director had Reverend Bermingham, the priest who consulted on the film, bless the set and comfort the cast and crew.

The stereotypical depiction of a Catholic exorcism is now firmly entrenched in popular culture, ever since the release of *The Exorcist*. Although this depiction is indeed one valid interpretation, exorcists are not always Catholic, nor have they been. Exorcism is not only a Catholic rite, or even Christian, for that matter. Almost all people have had some form of exorcism in their belief system. Some of the earliest exorcisms were performed by shamans, and in some parts of the world still are.

The Shaman Appears

The origin of shamanism runs parallel with the history of mankind. In prehistoric times, humans lived in an ecological connection with nature and depended for their survival on the way they could be open to nature, to orient themselves from four cardinal directions, listen to every sound, and to know weather patterns. Humankind's attention was mainly focused on their relationship with the environment, with plants and animals, and with their own life energy. They had to know which plants could heal and which made you ill or even dead. This was sacred wisdom; it meant the difference between life and death. The shaman was the guardian of the balance between the natural world, man, and the supernatural. He had the ability to make contact with the world of spirits and gods. He could bridge the boundary between Heaven and Earth, between past and future.

Although the word "shaman" initially occurred only in certain Siberian tribes, the term was used by anthropologists at the end of the nineteenth century for all people who fell into a trance and communicated with spirits. Although each culture has its own unique methods and techniques, a number of basic principles for traditional shamanism are consistent. The shamanic worldview is made up of three levels: the upper world or Heaven, the middle world or Earth, and the underworld or the lower world.

The image of the three worlds must not only be interpreted geographically, but also partly seen as a metaphor. The upper world is that of the angelic beings, of the spirits, of the deceased, and of the gods. The inhabitants of this world radiate wisdom and they give the visitor insight. The middle world concerns the earthly daily reality, comprising just matter. In the middle world, the present, the past, and the future coexist. The lower world consists of animalistic power and of the dead who have not traveled to the higher world.

In addition to this three-part cosmos, shamanistic cultures assume that everything around us is alive. Not only the human being and the animal, but also the plant, the stone, the chair, the Earth, and the stars. Everything has a soul and with everything a personal relationship is possible. Based on this view, everything and everyone is interconnected. The third principle of traditional shamanism is the belief in an existence after death, sometimes in reincarnation. It is assumed that in addition to the reality in which we live, an invisible reality exists, to which the shaman gains access by going into a trance. Shamans travel through the three worlds in search of knowledge, strength, and a better understanding of reality. A fourth characteristic of shamanism is the intensive and respectful relationship with nature and the forces of nature. Special forces are assigned to the surrounding nature, such as trees, rocks, rivers, and natural forces like wind, rain, and lightning. To the shaman, body, soul, and spirit are regarded differently but united as a single unit. Nature and the spiritual world are inextricably linked to this unity. Illness is seen as a disruption of the balance between man, nature, and spiritual world. The work of the shaman consists of restoring the balance between patient, nature, and the spiritual world.

Shamanic Exorcism

To the shaman, spirits are conscious, intelligent, and communicative beings who are invisible to ordinary people. Spirits roam around certain places in the everyday world, the upper world, and the lower world. There are spirits of nature, of the animals, of the deceased, and of the gods. Shamans can make contact with these beings and receive instructions from them on how they can best serve the community. When there was an illness, the shaman would diagnose the part of the human consciousness that can move outside matter, often referred to as a "dreambody." The dreambody is comparable to the etheric body, mental body, energy body, or the more familiar soul. Illness or health according to the shamanistic vision is determined by the state in which the dreambody is situated.

To make the diagnosis, the shaman enters a trance where he can view the patient's dreambody. He will often ask for assistance from a helper from the spiritual world. From this view, illness can have four causes. One, part of the dreambody may have disappeared due to a traumatic event. The sick person suffers from a loss of the soul. A second cause of illness consists of the invasion of energy from the outside into the dreambody: a possession. A third and fourth cause may be that a dreambody is too weak or out of balance.

The shamanic therapy is performed by the shaman. The shaman travels through the spiritual world to ask the spirits for advice and assistance. The shaman must get into a trance, a state of consciousness that can be evoked by meditating and listening to a monotonous sound such as drums, a drumroll, or a rattle. In addition to these rhythm instruments, hallucinogenic plants such as the South American plant ayahuasca or psilocybin mushrooms are sometimes used to travel. The shaman has a number of spirits that act as personal spiritual counselors. These spirits advise the shaman on the cause of illness and pain and give him directions for healing.

When an evil spirit or negative energy has possessed someone, the shaman will perform an exorcism by traveling to the spiritual world to find out what entity is tormenting the patient. The information about the cause usually comes in the form of shamanistic symbols. For example, an entity may manifest as an animal or an object that has lodged somewhere in the patient. The shaman removes the foreign force from the body by pulling it out, sucking it out, or removing it with certain hand movements. Sometimes, this does not work because the entity is too powerful, and the patient's soul is lost. In that case, the shaman makes a journey to the spiritual world to investigate where the lost parts of the soul are located. As soon as the shaman has recovered the soul, he takes it to reality. The lost soul is blown into the patient.

The Incas practiced something similar. The Incas believed that illness was a result of either a punishment from the gods or evil magic. In Inca medicine, medicine men believed that the body is surrounded by a shining energy field that is like a matrix of light. This energy field determines how we live, how we heal, and how we die. Every emotional, physical, or spiritual event, every trauma that one has experienced, can be read in the luminous energy field. The luminous energy field shows not only which diseases a person has, but also which diseases someone will receive. The treatment involves the cleansing of energy from the luminous energy field to prevent disease from manifesting.

Jesus: Shaman and Exorcist

It may sound strange at first, but some anthropologists consider Jesus a shamanic figure. Jesus performed both healing and exorcism, he influenced souls and emerged as a prophet and teacher who held great knowledge (Craffert, 2008). In the New Testament, the expulsion of demons, together with healing of the sick, the blind, and the lame, is an important activity of Jesus and his disciples. A rather confusing mythology about the Devil has been built up from various passages in the Bible. The story of the serpent in Paradise is identified with the Devil, who wants to tempt people into disobedience to God.

One story of Jesus performing an exorcism involves a man who was possessed by demons who came out of the city to meet Jesus. For a long time, he had not put on clothes, nor lived in a house. Seeing Jesus, he cried out, fell at his feet, and said in a loud voice, "What do you want with me, Jesus, Son of the Most High God? I beg you, do not make me suffer!" (Luke 8:28 KJV). Then, Jesus commanded the evil spirit to come out of this man.

For many times the spirit had seized him. He was tied with chains and irons on his feet, but he broke his bonds, and the demon dragged him to deserted places. Jesus asked him, "What is your name? The man replied, 'Legion,' for many demons had entered him" (Luke 8:30 KJV). The demons begged Jesus not to command them to go back to Hell. Close to where this was taking place, a herd of pigs were foraging for food on the hill. The demons begged Jesus to allow them to enter these pigs, and he agreed. Then, by Jesus's command, the demons flew out of the man and entered the pigs. From the top of the cliff, the possessed pigs "ran violently down a steep place into the lake and were choked" (Luke 8:33 KJV).

After seeing this, the guards got scared and ran away. They announced the news in the city and in the country, and people went out to see what had happened. When they came to Jesus, they found at his feet the man whom the demons had once possessed, now clothed and seemingly rational. The witnesses told them how the victim had been saved. The man who was saved by Jesus asked him to stay by his side, but Jesus sent him away saying, "Return to thine own house, and shew how great things God hath done unto thee" (Luke 8:39 KJV). The man went off and proclaimed throughout the whole city how Jesus had saved him from demons (ibid.).

With a long history of belief in demonic possession, it is interesting to note that in its early days, the Church linked exorcism to the baptism sacrament. Before being baptized, an aspiring Christian convert would submit to the so-called rite of exsufflation. This was a part of the baptismal ceremony in the ancient Church during which the Christian candidate stood with his hands stretched out toward the West (considered the place where the Devil dwells), clapped, and spit three times in defiance of Satan.

Until the beginning of the sixteenth century, there was no unified rite of exorcism. In 1523, Alberto Castellani published the book *Liber Sacerdotalis*, which Pope Leo X recognized as valid for the Catholic Church. After the changes in the ritual by Cardinal Santori, it was used until the year 1602. Santori set various criteria for the recognition of possession. At the end of this work in 1614, Pope Paul V published the *Rituale Romanum*, which is still valid. The book may be in effect longer than any before. The exorcism ritual of Pope Paul V was based on centuries of exorcists' experiences, which contributed to its constant relevance and is a reason why it has lasted so long in almost unchanged form. *Rituale Romanum* of 1614 saw minor improvements and additions in 1926 and 1952. On June 4, 1990, and then on February 12, 1991, the Church made a few updates to the exorcism ritual, but aside from those updates, this text remains the guidebook for the Roman Catholic exorcism ritual.

Dybbuk of Judaism

In Judaism, exorcism is understood as expulsion of a dybbuk. A dybbuk is the spirit of someone who did not lead a righteous way of life and, as a result, could not find peace in the afterlife. Because the spirit cannot go into the next world, it is forced to seek a new body. The expulsion of the dybbuk is carried out by a tzaddik. In the Hebrew Bible, the word "tzaddik" appears in Genesis when Abraham tries to save the righteous of Sodom and Gomorrah: "That be far from Thee to do after this manner, to slay the tzaddik with the rasha; and that the tzaddik should be as the rasha, that be far from Thee" (Gen. 18:25 Orthodox Jewish Bible). According to tradition, this name also serves as a title and designates a rabbi in Hasidism. This notion is then associated with that of miracle, the "charismatic" rabbis being endowed with supernatural powers. The Kabbalah attributed also to the tzaddik divine powers, including that of mediating between God and the Jewish people.

During an Orthodox Jewish exorcism rite, a group of ten adult males, referred to as a minyan, must be there to witness. The rite of exorcism is accompanied by the sound of a shofar, an ancient musical instrument traditionally made of a ram's horn. This is in reference to Yom Kippur, or the Day of Atonement, which is the holiest day of the year in Judaism. In addition to praying for atonement, funeral prayers are read for the evil spirit to go where it belongs, to cross over to the other side.

In *Antiquities of the Jews*, Josephus describes an exorcism carried out by a Jew named Eleazar. Eleazar performed an exorcism using his ring, which had Solomon's seal. He applied it to the possessed man's nose, and it drew out the demon. The man immediately fell to the ground, and Eleazar then told the demon never to return, calling the name of Solomon and reciting the spells. Descriptions of exorcism also exist in the rabbinical literature. Although some rabbinical literature mentions exorcism, it is difficult to judge how often the ritual of exorcism happened in antiquity because there are very few stories from this period. Most of the surviving stories date back to the sixteenth century, like the *Shoshan Yesod ha-'Olam* (Lily, Foundation of the World), which is the most comprehensive late medieval Hebrew magic text known to date. It contains techniques that promise to offer protection from injuries, doubts and fears, bad dreams, business negotiation problems, crying children, women having difficulty in labor, dangers of travel, and demonic afflictions.

In the Jewish tradition, where did demons come from? According to the Talmud, God was busy with the last details of creation on the day before the Sabbath. He was in the process of making new souls but had to stop working because on the Sabbath, he rested. This is why demons have no bodies, only spirits. But there were also those who possess both the soul and the body. There is a rabbinic legend that for 130 years after the expulsion from Eden, when Adam was separated from Eve, he had relationships with female demons whose children belong to this group. Demons have special tasks like the angels. They are associated with impurity, so it is important, for example, to wash hands to drive away demons. There are times when you are particularly vulnerable to demons, such as during the night, especially Wednesday and Saturday.

There is even an urban legend associated with this, known as the Dybbuk Box. In an article of July 25, 2004, the *Los Angeles Times* reported on a small wooden wine cabinet that had gone up for auction on eBay. It was put up for sale by the owner of a small antiques business in Portland, Oregon, who bought a box at an estate sale in 2003. According to the seller, the box had belonged to a Holocaust survivor named Havaleh who had escaped to Spain and purchased it on her way to the United States. Inside were two old pennies, locks of hair bound by a cord, a small statue engraved with the Hebrew word "Shalom," a small golden wine goblet, one dried rosebud, a single candleholder with four octopus-shaped legs, and allegedly, one dybbuk.

The store owner decided to give the dybbuk box to his mother for her birthday. After she got it, she suffered a stroke and lost her ability to speak. He then tried to give the box to other family members and friends, but they all eventually gave him back the box claiming that it smelled like cat urine and jasmine. All the people who got the box had the same nightmare in which their friends turned into demons and smashed them to death. The box is currently housed in a paranormal museum and was the inspiration for the 2012 film *The Possession.*

Jinn of Islam

Exorcism is not exclusive to Judeo-Christian theology. Exorcism in Islam is the expulsion, not of demons, but of genies, or jinn. The jinn are sometimes called "genies" in the Western popular culture. They are known primarily from the collection of fairy tales *Arabian Nights* and represented as magical spirits that take a form resembling a man with arms crossed in appearance but are trapped in lamps. A genie grants three wishes to whoever rubbed the magic lamp and awakened him. However, true jinn are not friendly Disney genies, nor do they look like a pink-chiffon-clad Barbara Eden from the '60s. Jinn are entities in Arab mythology that usually act as evil spirits.

Regardless of what I learned in my university courses, and no matter what research I may do now, because I was raised

Catholic, I see things through the lens of a Christian Westerner. In presenting information on jinn, it was important for me to make sure I was accurate about their portrayal, leaving any potential bias aside. I am also limited to English, French, and Latin. Many of the best sources are in Arabic, so I consulted my good friend Hakan Ogun, whom I consider the one of the foremost experts on the history and archaeological sites of Turkey. He explained to me that the jinn are intelligent energetic beings created from smokeless flame of fire before humankind were on Earth when the Earth was a fireball planet covered by lavas and volcanoes and hot gases, way before the creation of the seas and oceans. Hakan explains that jinn live in nations, like humans. They have tribal leaders known as demon kings.

According to Arabic mythology, the most powerful and evil of the jinn are the ifrits. Ifrits are believed to live in the underworld and sometimes lurk around ruins or caves. They are large, winged demons that bleed fire and seek to destroy the lives of human beings. They are known to attack women in particular in their search for a bride. Another type of jinn is the *goul. Gouls* are usually female, dwell in deserts and cemeteries, and dine on the flesh of a fresh corpse. Like the demons of Judaism and Christianity, jinn can be summoned through playing with cursed objects, amulets, or even Ouija boards.

The rite of exorcism, or expulsion of the jinn, is very similar to that of the Catholic Church. Some of the early signs of jinn possession are laziness, aggression, headaches, nightmares, sleepwalking, and laughing while asleep. When the person is fully possessed, they can no longer think for themselves and only follow the orders of the jinn. The person will obey the commands of the jinn at all times. At this stage of the possession, the jinn can cause physical harm to the possessed and leave bruises and injuries, including mysterious scratches. When it is determined that a person needs an exorcism, a clergyman who has received permission from a higher ecclesiastical authority reads special prayers and excerpts from the Quran, which are aimed at expelling the demon. This evil entity manifests itself in much the same way as Christian demons, and like them, they try to tempt, lie, and negotiate with the exorcist on how they will leave the body of the possessed person. The Islamic exorcism is called *Ruqyah*. I asked Hakan Ogun to explain *Ruqyah* further. He clarified that *Ruqyah* is made up of spells that are either written or spoken to drive the jinn out of the possessed. *Ruqyah* is a method of reciting certain verses and chapters of Quran for certain number of times, like reciting Sūrat An-Nās seven times and reciting Sura Al-Falaq seven times. Another method is to write those specific verses on papers in their original language and keep them in certain places or carry them like an amulet necklace. Hakan offers one word of caution, though: "*Ruqyah* is not a common method. A person should really know how to perform *Ruqyah* properly, otherwise people fall into the hands of charlatans" (Lynn-Ogun, interview, 2018). *Havvas* is the method of contacting the jinn, but this is very dangerous and even forbidden.

Dangers of Exorcism

Hakan made an important point. Exorcisms can be very dangerous. People are afraid of possession by demons, but the exorcism itself can sometimes be just as harmful. Exorcisms that do not end well are still regularly in the news.

- In 1995, priests of the Pentecostal movement in San Francisco during an attempt to drive out demons gave a woman so many strokes that she eventually died.

- In 1997, a woman was murdered in Glendale, California, and in New York City, a five-year-old girl

died after she was forced to swallow a mixture containing ammonia and vinegar, after which her mouth
was taped shut.

- In 1998 in upstate New York, a seventeen-year-old girl
  was suffocated by her mother with a plastic bag, in an
  attempt to kill the Devil she believed was inside her.

- In 2001, a thirty-seven-year-old woman in New
  Zealand was strangled by a priest during exorcism.

- In 2005, a priest and four nuns were charged because
  they had crucified another nun with a towel in her
  mouth. They thought she was possessed, but she
  turned out to be schizophrenic and died of dehydration and lack of oxygen.

Some of these stories come and go in the news and do not
receive the attention they maybe should. Not all of them end up as
source material for movies, but one particular case has. Take the
case of the German girl Anneliese Michel, who was an education
major at the University of Würzburg. Two films were made about
her ordeal: *The Exorcism of Emily Rose* (2005) and *Requiem* (2006).
As the story goes, in 1968, Anneliese was diagnosed with epilepsy.
She received medication for it, but her health continued to deteri-
orate. By 1970, she was admitted to a hospital for six months with
tuberculosis, where she became increasingly depressed. In June
1970, a neurologist found that her EEG showed abnormalities. A
week later she saw a malicious demon in a vision for the first
time. She used to pray long and intensely, but now she was afraid
to because she feared the demon would reappear.

In 1973 she continued to suffer from seizures and regularly
saw demonic faces with horns. She was tormented by the constant
smell of rotting flesh. Her father took her to the northern Italian

pilgrimage town of San Damiano, where Mary had appeared many times since 1964. While there, Anneliese fell to the ground, claiming her feet were burning.

People called in the help of Father Ernst Alt. He asked permission from a bishop to exorcise, but this was initially refused. Anneliese had meanwhile developed an aversion to sacred objects and would go into fits of rage when she saw them. She would become beastly and violent, sometimes growling like an animal. After Father Alt performed a small exorcism ritual in August 1974, she completely lost her temper. She tore the clothes off her body, urinated on the floor, ate spiders and coal, and physically attacked the priests. The demon who had taken possession of her called himself Judas.

By the end of September 1975, after their initial attempts failed to help Anneliese, the priests decided to perform a more intensive exorcism. The demons, who, including Judas, called themselves Lucifer, Nero, and Hitler, became increasingly violent with Anneliese. She would slam her head against the wall. She hardly slept, stopped eating, broke her knees after too many kneeling sessions, lost a massive amount of weight, and eventually died in July of 1976, one day after the sixty-seventh exorcism. The cause of death was malnutrition and dehydration. She weighed only seventy pounds. Her parents and the two priests in charge of the exorcism were convicted of negligent homicide. The grave of Anneliese has since become a place of pilgrimage, about which urban legends are now told.

Even though there are dangers, the demand for exorcisms has been on the rise in many countries. In Italy in particular, the number of exorcists increased in one fell swoop as the Vatican ordered each diocese worldwide to appoint at least one exorcist. To meet demand, a university course in Rome was developed to help teach priests the craft of exorcism. The course included guest lectures from theologians, psychologists, doctors, psychiatrists, and criminologists. The training provided the priests with knowledge about the historical, theological, sociological, and medical aspects of an exorcism. They also learned how to determine whether someone is possessed or not and how the Devil can be "defeated." The course was not only offered in Rome, but also in the United States. The Roman Catholic Church does not want to interfere with psychological ailments. A typical victim of demonic possession has often seen several doctors without any result. Those who do not always benefit from doctors often try something alternative. The exorcist can therefore be seen as an alternative healer. So first, a medical doctor or psychologist has to give the green light. Only then can a theological diagnosis be started. Exorcism rites may be relatively unchanged in religions like Judaism, Catholicism, Islam, and even Native American traditions, but there are many more faiths that conduct exorcisms in their own unique ways and put a twist or two on this ancient and almost universal tradition.

My Eyewitness Account of a Modern-Day Exorcism

When I was in my early twenties, I embarked on a cross-country journey to find answers to spiritual questions. I visited a diverse range of holy places and met hundreds of people from different faiths. I had many adventures—so many, I could write a whole book on just my spiritual quest, but for the current topic, I have only one story to share: my eyewitness account of a modern-day exorcism.

I was in a small town in South Carolina where the population was less than three hundred people. For such a sparsely populated area, there were a lot of churches. One evening, an acquaintance that I had made in while passing through invited me to attend a church service at a small Christian church on the outskirts of town. The road to the church was literally dirt. Had it not been for the intense humidity of that South Carolina summer night, the upheaval of the dust would have been like a smoke screen. Instead, it was like mud.

We approached the church, but this church looked more like a residential house retrofitted with a wheelchair ramp and a few stained-glass windows. There was no parking lot, so we pulled into a grassy field on the side of the building. My friend shut off the car and sat quietly. The awkward silence grew increasingly uncomfortable. Maybe I was just getting a little spooked because there were no lights in this field. I asked my friend how many people were expected tonight. She said, "the usual," only adding to the awkwardness. A light came on in the front of the building, and it was a beacon to everyone else who had apparently been waiting in their vehicles. We all got out and traversed the muddy field together, leading up to the side door of the church where we were met by a smiling preacher.

At the beginning of the evening, things seemed familiar enough. This was a Bible-based church whose members came from all over the rural area to worship together many times a week. The preacher spoke of Jesus's miracles, and the congregation sang hymns that I recognized from other Christian denominations, but it wasn't long before things became quite unfamiliar. About an hour into the gathering, the preacher became so exuberant that he leapt up onto the pews and began sprinting from one to the other. As he did this, some churchgoers started shaking, while others still started uttering strange words. After the preacher's unexpected outburst, he took his place up at the pulpit, lowered his head, and lifted his hands in prayer.

My eyes were focused on the preacher, still processing what I had just witnessed, when seemingly out of nowhere, a woman in a hospital bed appeared. She had been wheeled through a door across from the pulpit and left at the front of the church. From this point, things took an even stranger turn. The preacher stayed motionless at the pulpit while congregation members, including children as young as five, rolled on the floor speaking in tongues. The woman in the hospital bed looked as if she were asleep. She appeared weak and haggard, not elderly, but rather in her late forties or early fifties.

One by one, members of the group gathered around the bed. My friend and guide for the evening looked over at me and after having little to say until now, asked if I had anything to confess because they were about to do an exorcism. I was completely taken aback. To me, a former Catholic, an exorcism meant priests, crucifixes, heads spinning, and green projectile vomit. I was not sure why a confession would be in order at a time like this, but I didn't want to draw attention to myself, so I declined. Skeptical, albeit intrigued, I went up to get a closer look at what was happening, as I was one of only three people left sitting in the pews. Everyone else was up front, surrounding the woman in the hospital bed. The preacher put his hands over the woman and she spoke in tongues. She continued to moan and writhe, and from the same door where she was wheeled in came a procession of about four live goats. Yes, goats.

As the goats walked aimlessly through the church, the hospital bed shook violently. The woman in the bed shrieked, her face so red that I feared she would have a stroke. Her vocalization oscillated between glass-shattering shrieks and guttural growls. The only word that was intelligible was "Alu." The preacher asked, "Demon, is that your name?" To which the woman responded only, "Alu! Alu!"

The exorcism continued for another hour. Gradually, people grew quieter, some of the children falling asleep on the church floor. The preacher never left the woman's side. Then, as if waking from a fever-ridden sleep, the woman sat up and put her arms around the preacher and embraced him. When she pulled away from him, there was a clarity in her eyes that had not been there previously. The congregation members clapped and cheered, and all the while, goats still walked between pews.

The woman in the hospital bed got up and, with help from the others, walked into a meeting room adjacent to the main area where the exorcism had taken place. Everyone, including me, gathered in this meeting room where we were offered punch and cookies. There was a step-in bathtub used for baptisms. The preacher escorted the exorcised woman over to the tub and baptized her. The "after-party" continued for another hour or so, and the whole event took about four hours.

I look back at that night with only one regret. I had attended this ritual a few years before I went back to college to study anthropology, the parent field of archaeology. Thus, I was not equipped to properly study this ritual with the tools of an ethnographer, only that of a curious girl. As such, it was not until the car ride back to my hotel that I asked about the goats. The explanation given was that each goat was there to be the literal scapegoat. My friend went on to explain that the goats would be slaughtered and sacrificed to get rid of the demon that possessed the woman, and that the meat would be used in the food pantry or given to poor church members. As a vegetarian and animal lover, my heart grew heavy. I would not be in attendance for that part of the process, thankfully. I left the next morning to visit a Buddhist temple farther south.

Later, as I studied different aspects of ancient demonology, I came across a familiar name: Alû. Was this the same Alû that supposedly possessed the woman in the hospital bed? Alû is not a grammatically complex word, so it may have just been a common utterance, an easy combination of sounds. Nevertheless, there is a Sumerian demon named Alû. This dreadful demon has no limbs, no ears, and no face. He hovers over people at night as they sleep and binds their arms, legs, tongue, causing sleep paralysis, and ultimately, possessing people. Had the woman in South Carolina been bound to a hospital bed because of an ancient Sumerian demon? Was this all in her head? Had this been a case of mass hysteria? The woman survived the whole event (which is more than can be said for the goats), but how common is her experience? How safe is exorcism? My journey of discovery left me with more questions than answers.

Enter, Exorcist

It's been well over a decade since I witnessed that exorcism. I have since come to understand some of the things that took place. The goats, for example, are reminiscent of the story of Jesus performing an exorcism on a man and forcing the demons into a herd of pigs. These poor little animals were literal "scapegoats." Although I have studied religion and philosophy over the years, unresolved questions still linger. To help me understand exorcism in a more modern sense, I contacted my friend Bill Bean, a renowned exorcist and spiritual deliverance minister. Bill has performed hundreds of exorcisms all over the world. He describes himself as being anointed in the area of spiritual warfare and deliverance ministry, addressing anything from curses, blocks, attachments, obsession, and oppression to possession by demonic spirits. Bill is also a life coach who provides guidance and advice on how to be strong in mind, body, and spirit. With great sensitivity and understanding, Bill helps his clients to find solutions to a wide array of life challenges. He works with each client to help them build on their strengths to identify and achieve life goals.

Bill ministers to many who are going through problems with relationships, alcohol and drug addictions, sickness, depression, and those who feel that they have lost their way in life. You may recognize Bill from the Lifetime Movie Network, Discovery Channel, SYFY Channel, Travel Channel, Destination America, Animal Planet, Gaiam TV, Coast to Coast AM Radio, Beyond Belief, Cornerstone TV, Dead Files, the LMN series *I Was Possessed*, and others. The following is a transcript from my interview with Bill.

What is the difference between demonic oppression and possession?

BB: Oppression begins with a victim or victims being exposed to something through trauma such as child molestation and rape, along with other mental and physical abuses. Perhaps even a family bloodline curse could attract demons to a person if they happen to be in a depression or weakened emotional state. It can also take place when a person decides to invoke by the use of a Ouija board, séance, provoking or inviting a spirit in. Even if demonic spirits are attached to a house or to land, they could still be attracted to a person who is on a lower frequency due to emotional distress.

All life operates on frequency and vibration, and if we operate on high frequency, high vibration, then life is good, and we are moving forward. However, if a person is on low frequency and vibration, then life is not good, and it's as if a black cloud is over that person's head. Once in that state of existence, the Devil and his demons will aid and abet in a variety of situations (including paranormal/supernatural activity) aimed at tearing the victim down to the point of exhaustion, hopelessness, despair, suicidal thoughts, and just plain giving up!

When the will to live along with the will to fight is relinquished, then a full demonic possession can take place. When a person is under demonic oppression, they are still aware of what is taking place, but when a person comes under a full demonic possession, they have no idea of what is taking place when the demonic force is activated within them. This is not to say that a constant total memory loss takes place, but when demons manifest through the victim, it's as if that person's mind has been unplugged and the invading demonic force has plugged in. I have seen it many times in my life and throughout my career as an exorcist. The key to keeping demons far away is to make God first and to have strong faith. I call it "warrior mode," which is walking in strong faith, strength, and courage every day. That keeps our frequency and vibration on high, which keeps the Devil at bay.

How can you tell if someone is possessed?

BB: For me, I have been given holy discernment by God. I don't claim to be anything or to have superpowers, but God's power works very strongly through me. *He* gives me a knowing of things. One of the gifts that I have is the ability to look into a person's eyes and see beyond them. I have literally seen demons behind the eyes of some people at first glance. Other indicators of possession are the victim feeling of a bad spirit around them; listening to demonic music; developing severe anger and rage issues; developing a compulsion to wear black clothing every day; developing an obsession with death, destruction, and fire; having night terrors; a feeling of isolation, depression, hopelessness; lack of faith; being turned off to God and Jesus; acting out of character; withdrawing from family and friends; seeing UFOs and/or aliens; using drugs and drinking heavily; not wanting to shower or bathe; hearing voices (internal and external); redness or dark circles around the eyes (I have seen several victim's eyes go all white, all black, all red and yellow, with reptilian slits in them).

Other indicators are: Talking in other voices; talking in a very deep voice; sudden psychic abilities; superhuman strength; growling; hissing; violently attacking people; cursing at God, Jesus, and holy men; the ability to levitate; threats to kill and curse others; the ability to summon more demons; the ability to make light bulbs blow and to drain power from the home and from people. They also might foam at the mouth, bite people, spit at people, scream and screech at inhuman decibels. Demons will also shout at and threaten the exorcist. I have personally heard voices coming from victims saying things such as, "She's ours and you can't have her. F*** you, get away from us. God can't have her. She's ours," followed by cackling and/or deep laughter. In one case, the demonic force speaking through the victim recited Bible scriptures, one after the other in a mocking way! The victim didn't know any Bible scripture at all.

Have you ever seen anyone levitate, speak in other languages, or shape-shift?

BB: Yes, I have seen victims levitate, speak in other languages, and shape-shift!

You say that "it only takes an little opening in the door" to let in an entity. Could that opening be an object? Can objects harbor evil spirits or demons?

BB: Yes, it sure could. I say a blessing over every single thing that comes into my home. I don't care if it's brand-new or not! It's super important to be aware that demonic forces can be attached to people, places, and things.

I have encountered many cursed objects and have seen people come under demonic oppression as a result. People who collect antiques should be very careful because you never know if something evil might be attached. It's best to pray over the objects before bringing them into your home. I would never move into a home unless I blessed it beforehand. I travel nonstop all over America, and I bless every hotel room that I stay in, along with every vehicle that I rent.

You also mention Jesus saying, "In order to receive, you must believe." Could this go for demons, as well? Must you believe in demons to become possessed?

BB: No, I have helped people from other faiths who were possessed. I recall performing an exorcism for a family in Cairo, Egypt. One of the daughters was possessed, and God worked through me to free her.

Have you noticed an increase in demonic activity over the years?

BB: I have noticed a very large increase in demonic activity over the last three years.

In your lectures, you've said that in 1995, you started seeing UFOs when you traveled to and from work. Do you think that there is a connection between demons and UFOs?

BB: Yes, I sure do. When I began being "contacted" by UFOs in 1995, I felt that I was being observed at times, threatened at other times, and protected as well. I feel that some, if not the majority of the encounters and experiences, were demonic in nature, designed to destroy me. I also had many divine encounters between 1995 and 2008, but I know that God's angels protect me from all harm. It's my strong belief that the Devil had been on a mission to destroy me since a child because he did not want me to be where I'm at now, helping others for God.

What are your thoughts on the abduction phenomenon? Is it possible that so-called alien abductions are really demons attempting to possess people?

BB: It's possible, yet I have other feelings about it. Suppose it were connected, yet for a different purpose. I cannot prove what I'm about to say, yet in my humble opinion perhaps the alien abduction phenomenon is geared toward harvesting.

I do know this: High levels of stress, fear, and trauma cause the pineal gland and adrenal glands to produce secretions. It's been reported that those secretions produce one of the most powerful drugs known to man, adrenochrome. Is this drug being harvested from victims and sold for large amounts of money on the black market? I don't know for sure, but it surely wouldn't surprise me. Are the eggs being harvested from women as well? I don't know for sure, but I have heard many stories about that as well.

I love how you say you need to get into "warrior mode" to defend yourself against evil. Can you explain how people can start to do this?

BB: It all begins with having a close and personal relationship with God. If we make God first and follow the path of Jesus, then great favor and many blessings will be the result!

Warrior Mode = Faith, Strength, and Courage

What is your most important advice to people on how they can protect themselves against malevolent forces?

BB: Follow these ten simple steps and the Devil and his minions will flee from you:

1. Make God first.

2. Follow the path and the teachings of Jesus.

3. Build your faith.

4. Forgive.

5. Find your purpose in life.

6. Use the power of positive thinking.

7. Set goals.

8. Give to others.

9. Be grateful for everything.

10. Walk in faith, strength, and courage: warrior mode!

It is easy to see how "warrior mode," as Bill describes it (walking in faith, strength, and courage), would be a helpful way to navigate life, regardless of your faith. With all of the diversity in beliefs about demons and their possible power, there are many similarities between them. One common factor in most cases of possession is the idea that the possessed people brought about the possession themselves. Is this just some outdated version of "victim blaming," or could there be ways that people invite evil entities into their lives either unknowingly or unknowingly? More often than not, stories of possession seem to be linked to a material object, whether it is a Ouija board, dybbuk box, or cursed amulet. These cursed objects act as a gateway to the other side, but can material objects really contain evil? Likewise, can objects that are considered good, like a crucifix, actually protect us from evil entities?

CHAPTER 8

The Object
of Your Affliction

It's a familiar trope: A priest holds a crucifix in front of a possessed person, a vampire recoils at the sight of garlic, but can objects that are considered good truly protect us from evil entities? People have used inanimate objects as protection since antiquity. Amulets and talismans were also sought after, mostly for their portability; they were small enough to be worn or carried in a pocket. An amulet protects the wearer from diseases, curses, and other evils a person may encounter. A talisman, on the other hand, brings the holder happiness, health, wealth, and success. Although different, both amulets and talismans are worn around the neck and usually made of natural materials, like metals or stones. They can also be small, simple pendants packed with a spell written on a piece of paper or special herbs, like the one worn by Mia Farrow in the 1968 film *Rosemary's Baby.* Many different cultures use amulets and talismans. The Egyptians put amulets between the bandages of mummies, often depicting the ankh symbol. As a hieroglyph, the ankh means "life." Although there is still discussion about the exact meaning, the ankh was believed to give its owner a long life and sometimes also an eternal life—a life as god. The *wadjet*, or the eye of Horus, was and still is very popular. It is believed to have healing powers and to deter demons. The amulet was usually worn on the neck, arm, fingers, or ears, but could also be carried in a pocket or attached to a diseased part of the body.

If Looks Could Kill

Amulets are protectors against the "evil eye," a term used in the mythology and history of many cultures. The evil eye can mean different things to different people but is generally a type of curse.

The eye of Horus amulet represented the son of Osiris. In the story, Osiris was attacked by Seth, his wicked uncle. Seth stands for all evil while Osiris and his son symbolize good. Seth chopped Horus's eye into a number of pieces, but the god Thoth managed to restore the eye. Thus, the eye of Horus took on a protective function for the wearer and his health and eventually became a popular defender against the evil eye.

The human eye has been an intriguing symbol to man. The Celts, for example, had a giant demon monster named Balor who had an eye in the middle of his forehead. When he would open this eye, it would kill people. This is thematically similar to the Roman creature Medusa, who could turn people to stone with just one look. Although creatures of mythology have these supernatural attributes associated with the eye, some cultures believe that humans do too and can curse others just by staring at them long enough. Italians will sometimes put a red cornicello or *cornetto* (Italian for "little horn") in their car or wear one as a form of jewelry to protect against the evil eye, which they call *malocchio*.

In Turkey and in many other countries in the Middle East, you will find the *nazar*, a blue eye symbol. In the Middle East, it is commonplace to attach the *nazar* to clothing or hang it from the rearview mirror of a car. The *nazar* is now often made of blue-colored glass styled in the shape of a drop and sold in souvenir shops. In this part of the world, blue or green eyes are relatively rare, so the ancients believed that people with light eyes, particularly blue eyes, could curse you with just one look. This belief is so ancient, even the Assyrians had turquoise and blue-eye amulets. How ancient, scholars still debate, but the evil eye could be one of the most ancient curses in human history.

A typical *nazar* amulet made of handmade glass.

There are two specific Sumerian spells that are supposed to protect someone from the evil eye. One of the texts describes blue eyes as being filled with lapis lazuli, which scholars have interpreted to mean that it was used to protect against a curse (Kotzé, 2017). Lapis lazuli was commonly used in the ancient Near East as protection. But blue wasn't the only eye color associated with evil. Although a bit uncommon, people in the Middle East can certainly be born with blue eyes. It would not have been impossible for someone to encounter a blue- or green-eyed person. However, red was also mentioned in these Sumerian texts, which is interesting because a true red eye color is not known in humans. It's true that some albinos may appear to have reddish eyes in photographs, but they do not actually have red eyes; their lack of pigment allows the redness of their blood vessels behind the eyes to show. Thus, the Sumerians seemingly feared red eyes, most likely because they considered them a reptilian feature. In fact, both Sumerian texts begin by associating snakes with the evil eye:

Igi muš-ḫuš igi lu₂-ulu₃ muš-ḫuš

igi lu₂ nig-ḫul dim-ma muš-ḫuš

Translation: The eye (is in the shape of) a red snake, the eye of the man (is) a red snake, the eye of the evil man is a red snake" (ibid.). Archaeologists have also discovered Mesopotamian art predating the Sumerian texts that warn against the evil eye, which suggests that the belief is not just ancient, but prehistoric. (Van Buren, 1955)

Red is also an important color in Jewish mysticism. The protective thread in Kabbalah is an amulet of ordinary red wool thread, which is attached to the wrist of the left hand. The esoteric movement of Kabbalah originated in the Middle Ages, and over time it gained huge popularity, which still exists. According to the teachings of Kabbalah, the red thread is designed to protect the person wearing it against illness, envy, and demons. This belief originated in the legend of Lilith who, according to Kabbalah, was Adam's first wife. The story goes that Lilith and Adam argued a lot, and she eventually turned into an evil demon and left her husband. When Lilith flew over the Red Sea, she was caught by angels sent by God who were trying to bring her back to Adam. The angels told her that they would imprison her for eternity. They gave her only one chance at freedom, but to take it, she had to promise to spare any child her wrath if they were found wearing an amulet bearing the names of the angels. Now, anytime Lilith sees a child wearing a protective amulet, she remembers her promise to the angels and does not harm the child for fear of execution. Yet, some of the details of the legend changed, making it so that an amulet would be protective if it had Lilith's name on it. Another story has the prophet Elijah coming face to face with Lilith and demanding that she divulge her many names so that people could recognize her and thereby receive protection. She gave him a list of names, including Odem, which meant "redness" in Hebrew. Henceforth, the followers of the teachings of Kabbalah considered that the color red could guard against Lilith. In the early Middle Ages, Lilith was considered a dominant female demon, which led to her association as the wife and queen of Asmodeus, King of Demons (Sabbath, 2009).

Figures of protective demons were also placed in homes, buildings, or buried under a structure's foundation to safeguard people from evil spirits. Archaeologists refer to this as "ritual concealment." The practice of hiding magico-religious objects or even symbols for spiritual protection and good luck has been documented throughout history in almost every part of the world. Even now, some real estate agents believe that burying a statue of Saint Joseph in the yard of a house they are trying to sell will bring them luck. Lucky charms are everywhere in folklore, but if inanimate objects can have helpful or positive power, then inanimate objects could also be harmful or cursed. Cursed objects have been said to act as a gateway to the other side. The question remains, can objects really contain evil?

Cursed Objects

Although it is not surprising, it is unfortunately common that tourists will try to steal artifacts from archaeological sites. What may be surprising is that the tourists visiting the ruins of Pompeii have tried to steal relics or artifacts but often voluntarily return them or turn themselves in to the authorities. Some have sent notes apologizing for the theft, claiming that the artifacts are cursed. Archaeologist and director of the Pompeii site, Massimo Osanna, issued a public statement about the phenomena to Italian newspaper *La Corriere della Sera,* which explained that sometimes the thieves just regret their actions and feel guilty, but acknowledged that in recent years, the curators of Pompeii have received hundreds of packages of the stolen artifacts because, as the accompanying letters would say, those objects were responsible for harm to the relic thieves and their families (Brandolini, 2015). Could such curses be real? It seems more believable, perhaps, for relics from more romantic sites like Pompeii to be cursed. It adds to the mystery and mystique of the site. However, many people have claimed that everyday objects harbor negative energies, including decorative items, paintings, dolls, jewelry, and even a set of bunk beds!

The "Everyday" Curse

Many cursed object stories have roots in the early modern era, a time when what historians call the "consumer revolution" had firmly taken hold of the minds and hearts of the general public. You could say they became obsessed with material things, particularly consumer goods like home furnishing, paintings, jewelry, and even toys. It may be that the things we encounter in our everyday lives hold some sort of power over us. The following stories are from folklore and urban legends, which explains why they involve everyday objects.

The Basano Vase

The Basano vase kills everyone who tries to claim it as their own. According to legend, this seemingly innocuous silver vase was given to a bride on the eve of her wedding near Napoli, Italy—a wedding she would not live to see, as she died that very night still clutching the vase. The vase was passed down her family line for centuries, but anyone who took possession of it died not long after. The family eventually put the vase in storage. It was lost to time until 1988 when someone rediscovered it, along with a little parchment note that read, "Beware . . . This vase brings death." The new owner had no interest in keeping the vase, so he put it up for auction at an estate sale. He excluded the note from the item's description, however. A local pharmacist placed the winning bid and became the first person to display the vase in nearly five hundred years. He died within three months from an unknown cause.

His family then sold it to a skeptical surgeon who scoffed at the idea of the vase being cursed. The surgeon died within three months from an unknown cause. Finally, the vase was sold to an archaeologist who dated it to the fifteenth century. Sadly, the archaeologist died three months later of a mysterious infection. The archaeologist's family was so angry about the vase, now believing in the rumors, that they threw it out of the window! Supposedly, the vase came close to hitting a policeman who was patrolling below. The policeman fined the family for disorderly conduct and told them to come get their vase. They refused. They accepted the ticket and told him he could take the vase. The policeman then tried to offer the vase to a few local museums, but they all refused. The police ended up burying the vase in an undisclosed location.

The Crying Boy

Bruno Amadio, painter of the famous portrait of a little boy who cries, became a commercial success after his painting became very popular in the 1950s, as prints of the photo were mass-produced. This led to many people having one of these creepy prints in their homes. You may even remember having one in your childhood home, or maybe a grandparent's attic, like mine growing up (nightmare fuel for a kid). These pictures remained popular, but something strange started happening in the 1980s. A house burned down but left in the ashes was the crying boy painting, unharmed. People thought that was maybe just a little eerie, but then other people began reporting the same thing. Even firefighters could attest to the phenomenon. People started believing that the photo was cursed or even demonic. Another belief about this painting was that the image of the grieving child actually caused the fires. For years the stories of the unburned paintings were written off as urban legends, until the BBC researched the story only to discover that it was true! The paintings did survive, as they were covered with fire-retardant varnish!

Thomas Busby's Stoop Chair

In 1702, a drunken Englishman named Thomas Busby quarreled over a bad business deal with his father-in-law, Daniel Auty. He ended up killing Auty, and as a result, he was hanged at Sandhutton crossroads, beside a local inn, which changed its name to the Busby Stoop Inn. Yet, this was not the end of Busby's tale. Before he died, he looked over the spectators and warned everyone not to sit in his favorite chair at the inn, and that if they did, he could haunt or even kill them. In the years following his execution, people did indeed try to sit in Busby's chair, many of whom claimed they could feel the curse. In the 1970s, the chair was linked to a few freak accidents, so the owners of the inn decided to hang it from the ceiling of Thirsk Museum to prevent anyone from sitting in it ever again. Eventually, a historian carefully examined the chair and dated it to 1840; 138 years *after* Busby's hanging. The chair was not as old as it was once thought. The spindles on the chair were mass-produced by being machine-turned rather than using a pole lathe from the seventeenth century, as they would have when Busby was alive. Another case closed.

The Myrtles Plantation Mirror

In the nineteenth century, an American slave girl named Chloe was raped by her slave master, as was sadly often the case. Once he tired of her, he had planned to send her back out to work the fields of his Southern plantation. Chloe overheard him planning this, and when she was caught eavesdropping, the evil slave master punished her by cutting her ear. To hide her now mutilated head, she had to wear a turban. After years of abuse, she concocted a plan to poison the family, but the poison only worked on the mistress and her two young children, leaving Chloe riddled with guilt. She confessed to her fellow slaves, and out of fear, they decided to hang Chloe. Legend has it that poor Chloe is still haunting the old plantation house. She has appeared in photos and in mirrors, along with the spirits of the mistress and her two poisoned children.

The Possessed Bunk Beds

In the 1980s, a woman bought a set of used bunk beds from a thrift shop for her children when they were old enough. Because they didn't need them right away, her husband stored them in the cellar. After a few years, her children were old enough to have a bunk beds, so they moved them out of the cellar and into the children's room. Not long after, the children became seriously ill. Then, strange things started happening in the house. Furnishings would move on their own, the radio randomly turned on and off, and the children began having nightmares. They would wake up screaming that they had seen a witch. The parents asked their priest to come to bless the beds. Just as they thought things were better, the children's father came home from work one day and heard a voice say, "Come here." He followed the voice to the garage and saw that the garage was on fire so he ran to get a fire extinguisher. Upon returning to the garage, fire extinguisher in hand, there was no fire. The family had had enough. They set the bunk beds on fire and at last were at peace.

The Letta Me Out Doll

A man in Brison, Australia, noticed an old house in the neighborhood that he thought looked haunted. He went under the house with a flashlight and found one of the creepiest-looking dolls ever just lying there grinning at him. He took the doll with him, thinking maybe he could sell it to an antiques dealer. He thought it might be worth money because it was clearly handmade and had real human hair. He later had it studied at the Australian Museum in Sydney, where they determined by looking at the nails in the bottom of its shoes that it was two hundred years old and brought to Australia from Eastern Europe. The man found an interested antiques dealer who offered to buy the doll, but when he tried to deliver it, he became unable to move when he tried to lift the doll. He kept the doll and named it "Letta Me Out!" To this day, people are afraid of the doll, and dogs even try to attack it. It has been blamed for numerous paranormal incidents, including exploding lights.

Mandy the Doll

A porcelain doll known as Mandy, made in 1910, was said to have driven its owners to the brink of insanity. At night, she screamed and made wretched sounds as she hovered around the house. As a result, the family gave the doll to the Quesnel Museum in British Columbia, Canada. This didn't stop Mandy. In the museum, the staff reported that they heard Mandy's footsteps in the room where she was locked. Things would go missing at the museum, and items would be rearranged. Rumor circulated that this was Mandy's doing. Many visitors started to complain their cameras malfunctioned when they tried to take Mandy's photograph, and any attempt to put Mandy in a display with another doll would end in the other doll being thrown out of the display and broken. Obviously, Mandy does not like to share.

The Florentine Diamond

The Florentine Diamond is a huge yellow diamond weighing in at 137 carats. It was blamed for a string of notable deaths throughout history, including Queen Elizabeth I, King Farouk of Egypt, and Maximilian of Austria, and some say even the death of King Louis XVI and Marie Antoinette. Legend has it that the wife of Archduke Ferdinand, Sophie, was wearing the Florentine Diamond at the time she was assassinated. Thus, some have blamed it for starting World War I.

Believed to be one of the oldest diamonds known to man, it was carved by Lodewyk van Bercken for Charles the Bold. The diamond was worn by Charles when he died during the Battle of Nancy. When the battle zone was cleared, it was said that the diamond was uncovered and mistaken for a little piece of glass. A local picked it up and sold it. Eventually, the diamond ended up in the hands of the Grand Duke of Tuscany. The duke showed it to his friend Jean Baptiste Tavernier, a traveler and expert on jewels. The Florentine Diamond continued to be passed along to different nobles until it vanished. To this day, no one knows where the Florentine Diamond is. Maybe it, like so many cursed artifacts, has been hidden so that no one else may be harmed.

Mirror Arpo

This antique mirror is in a massive frame of gilded mahogany. It was rumored that the mirror maker was an occultist from the eighteenth century who used the mirror for séances. The mirror was repeatedly resold because several of its former owners died of a stroke or mysteriously disappeared without a trace. All in all, this sinister mirror claimed thirty-eight victims, one of whom was the Greek banker Kirakos. In 1769, he bought the mirror as a birthday gift for his sister. When he arrived with the mirror, his sister was nowhere to be found. A few days later, the banker and his coachman had disappeared, leaving behind a carriage in the forest still holding the mirror. The mirror found its way to a twenty-three-year-old named Laura Noel, who soon died of a cerebral hemorrhage.

Many years later, in Paris the cursed relic allegedly appeared in the estate of the Marquis de Fornaroli. On September 10, 1943, the marquis held an extravagant party to which he had invited high-ranking Nazis. The marquis's wife, at the height of the feast, retired to her bedroom and did not go back downstairs for the remainder of the night. When her worried husband went up to the second floor to check on his wife, the marquise was not there. Rather, in front of the mirror were an open lipstick and powder compact, a pearl necklace, and one of the marquise's shoes. In the corner, a chair was knocked over and on the wooden panels framing the mirror there were traces of fingernail scratches! The marquise was never seen again. SS-Hauptsturmführer Franz Schubach, who was interested in mystical and occult artifacts took the mirror out of the country.

Some explanations that were offered for the deadly, yet mysterious, powers of the mirror are that the mirror can reflect light in such a way that it affects the human brain and leads to a stroke. Another attempt to explain the mirror's murderous capability is that old mirrors used to be covered with an amalgam of a high concentration of mercury, which is deadly, and this could have been what caused instant death to anyone who touched it. The problem with that theory, however, is that although mirrors, and indeed most very old antiques, were coated in various neurotoxins, it would still take at least five to ten years to cause death.

So, what about the numerous disappearances? Some paranormal researchers have suggested that all those who disappeared moved to a parallel dimension on the other side of the mirror glass, like in the book *Alice's Adventures in Wonderland*. I think it will remain a mystery, as the mirror has itself now disappeared.

The Woman from Lemb

The Woman from Lemb was believed to be a limestone statue discovered in 1878 in Lemb, Cyprus. Known as the "The Goddess of Death" due to its resemblance to an ancient fertility goddess, it was believed to be dated to around 3500 BCE. The statue's owner was a British gentleman named Lord Elphont. After having the stature for nearly six years, his entire family had died unexplained deaths. Lord Elphont gave the statue away to his friend Lord Thompson-Noel, who also died along with his entire family shortly after accepting the gift.

Sir Alan Biverbrook assumed ownership of the statue, but he, his wife, and their two daughters suddenly and mysteriously died. Sir Biverbrook's sons survived and donated the statue to the Royal Scottish Museum in Edinburgh, where it supposedly remains today. As the tale goes, soon after its being displayed in the museum, the curator suddenly died of unknown causes. It is said that the museum locked the statue under glass, so that no one could touch it.

Was this statue cursed? The story has made its way around the world, but the truth is, *The Woman from Lemb* statue is definitely not cursed, nor was it responsible for anyone's death. Despite a great deal of Internet infamy, the statue is actually a legitimate archaeological artifact known as *The Lemba Lady*. It has been part of the collection of the Cyprus Museum in

Nicosia since it was discovered in 1970. It also has not killed anybody (so far).

The Burden of Proof

It seems that a physical object that was in some way involved in the beginning of the ordeal is a common element to many stories of possession. Can material objects contain evil? According to exorcist Bill Bean, cursed objects have indeed caused demonic oppression of some of the people he has encountered. He warned that collectors should be very careful because something evil might be attached to antiques they bring home. Upon learning this, I got a little worried. I happen to be an antiques collector, and one of the most recent additions to my collection is a 140-year-old wooden pendulum clock. Every time it strikes, it sounds like the ghost of Scrooge's old partner Jacob Marley is about to show up in his rattling chains. It was creepy before, but after speaking with Bill, I am beginning to have second thoughts about that old clock. I think I'll leave it unwound for a while, at least until after I'm finished writing this book!

Would there be any way that I could find out if my old clock is harboring some malevolent energy? Sure, I could have a psychic or medium look at it, but what about science? Contemporary paranormal researchers use a variety of tools to investigate in a more scientific way. Ghost hunters are becoming quite advanced in their quest to prove the existence of spirit entities. Cameras are basic, but important, tools in ghost hunting. They are usually equipped with an infrared function to enable night shooting. With these cameras, investigators are able to film in complete darkness. In addition to capturing visual evidence, an audio recording device is used to pick up both passive and active sound recordings. Another relatively simple tool is a thermometer, including an infrared thermometer. However, this is only suitable for measuring surface temperatures. Thermometers are believed to detect the temperature changes usually associated with the presence of a spiritual entity. A person sometimes claims to feel a cold spot on their arms or neck and may even feel as though they were touched.

In addition to these more conventional tools, some people try to detect the paranormal with a ghost box. A ghost box is a modified portable AM/FM radio that continuously scans radio frequencies in an attempt to pick up sounds from "the other side." Because the change from one frequency to the next can take place in less than a second, it is not likely that the listener would perceive coherent phrases or even words from a particular station. One of the more advanced tools used to detect entities are EMF meters, which detect electromagnetic fields; this tool is directly related to the theory that entities could manifest in energy form. A REM pod uses a telescopic antenna to generate its own EMF field and then sounds an alarm if this field is disturbed. This will determine if any spirits are in the vicinity of the REM pod. It's like an alarm system that can be placed at hot spots to sound the alarm during an investigation.

As a historian, archaeologist, and open-minded skeptic, I have a limited knowledge of what it might take to really find out if there is an evil presence in an object or place. So, I decided the best person to ask would be my friend Mike Ricksecker, author of the historic paranormal books *Ghosts of Maryland, Ghosts and Legends of Oklahoma, Campfire Tales: Midwest, Ghostorian Case Files: Volume 1,* and the *Encounters with the Paranormal* series. Mike has appeared on multiple television shows and programs as a paranormal historian, including Animal Planet's *The Haunted* and Biography Channel's *My*

Ghost Story, and *Coast to Coast AM with George Noory.* He produces a number of his own Internet shows, including *Ghosts and Legends, Paranormal Roads, The Edge of the Rabbit Hole Livestream Show,* and *Inside the Upside Down* on the Haunted Road Media YouTube channel.

With more than twenty-five years of involvement in the paranormal, Mike serves as a paranormal investigator and "ghostorian" with Society of the Haunted, and he regularly travels to speak about the paranormal and writing. I interviewed Mike to ask him what he thought about the possibility of cursed objects, as well as his thoughts on possession and the science behind the paranormal. The following is the transcript of our interview. Be prepared, as Mike is about to take you to the edge of the rabbit hole.

For background, can you tell me a little about yourself?

MR: I've always been interested in all things mysterious and started writing mystery fiction, historic fiction, and ghost stories when I was in the second grade, but my first paranormal experience that set me on my current path occurred when I was about eight or nine years old. I awoke late one night to a dark figure in the corner of my bedroom, what I thought at the time to be an intruder. It was certainly an intruder, but not the kind to which my young mind immediately flashed, a thief in the night. No, this person was completely dark and devoid of any noticeable characteristics.

I tried to scream and couldn't, and then it then proceeded to do something unforgettable. It approached me, leaned over my bed, and crossed my arms across my body. Still, at that close distance I could not make out any features, and still nothing came out of my mouth as I tried to scream. The thing then relented and ran off down the hall, opened a hallway closet door, and disappeared inside. I finally found my voice and my feet and ran off to my parents' bedroom.

From that experience alone, I knew there was something more to this world that we normally couldn't see or interact with, and the subject continued to fascinate me. I read books by Hans Holzer, developed a desire to seek out the truth about the Amityville house when I was a young teen, and had my first paranormal investigation when I was a sophomore in high school. Coupled with my writing, which transformed from pure mystery fiction to the more historical-based paranormal stories and experiences I write today, I was well on the journey.

Would you consider hauntings the same as possession? Or are they two very different concepts?

MR: Hauntings and possessions are two different concepts, and although many believe one may lead to the other, these are really two different paths.

A haunting occurs when an earthbound spirit lingers at a location and expresses itself through some sort of activity. This activity could be physical, such as moving objects across a room, opening and closing doors, or even a physical manifestation of a corporeal form. It could also be audible, such as a disembodied voice. Of course, a haunting could consist of both of these things.

Just for clarification, there are some "hauntings" that I don't consider hauntings at all although many others refer to these incidents as "residual haunts." These types of manifestations are like a playback of a scene from long ago and portray zero recognition of those that are observing them. Many have heard the tales of ghosts that walk through spots in a wall that used to be a doorway. This may be deemed paranormal activity, but I don't actually consider it a haunting because it's just a playback of a moment in time.

Possession occurs when a supernatural entity, usually a demon, enters and controls a human being. As a rule of thumb, and for simplicity's sake, we generally look at the following stages in the path to possession:

Infestation: This is the stage that most resembles a haunting. The demon has entered the home and is causing havoc therein.

Oppression: Mental attacks begin on a person, although there may be some physical attacks as well. In what may seem like a short period of time, a person will experience one or more of the following: frequent nightmares; frequent illnesses; struggles with employment, financial, and relationship issues; deep depression and states of anxiety.

Obsession: The targeted person loses many abilities to function normally and becomes preoccupied with thoughts about demonic activity. Sleep becomes nearly impossible, and thoughts of suicide may become prevalent.

Possession: This is the stage in which the demon has virtually taken control of its chosen host. Although the person does still have free will, he or she is so physically, emotionally, and mentally compromised that his or her ability to act upon that free will is extremely difficult, and the demon is able to act through the victim.

In addition to places, do you think objects can become possessed?

MR: Demons don't necessarily possess objects; they possess people, but they can attach themselves to objects and affect those who come into contact with those items. Some may view these as "cursed" objects because the demon comes along with it and begins infesting the location to which it's brought.

Are there tools that you use in your research that can detect evil entities?

MR: The electronic tools in my arsenal don't necessarily detect evil, but we can use them to collect data that will aid in making a determination as to whether or not a particular entity is evil in nature. We'll take the information we've gathered from our investigations via video cameras, audio recorders, electromagnetic field detectors, motion detectors, and temperature gauges, combine it with the interviews we've conducted and historic research of a location, and begin an assessment. This usually leads to additional research at the library and other literary sources such as historic maps and texts, and down the rabbit hole we go.

Some of the feedback we get through our recorded data will alert us that we may be dealing with a particularly nasty entity, such as a voice stating it wishes to do someone harm. There are other times in which the tool of the human body becomes useful, and that internal alarm system lets us know that something is not right in a particular area. If we happen to feel a heavy air of oppression in a particular room, we will concentrate our efforts there, and we are usually not disappointed in the results.

Can you tell me about a time are you felt such a strong evil presence you were actually afraid?

MR: When we filmed for our episode on *The Haunted,* we had been dealing with a malevolent human entity at a house in

Edmond, Oklahoma, for several months, and the family wanted it eradicated. Even though it wasn't a demon, demonologist Carl Johnson was called in to lead the cleansing of the home. The family was asked to stay outside during this process; however, their adult daughter, who had been the primary target of the activity, entered the home to use the restroom.

Over the course of years, she had been terrorized in her bedroom by an entity with red eyes, and during our investigations prior to the cleansing, I had witnessed the manifestation of a black mass in her bedroom, almost cloud-like in nature.

We found her in the master bedroom talking to something unseen at one end of the room. She was calling it out and demanding to know why it was frightening her, her family, and even the pets of the home. Carl decided to perform a blessing over the young woman, and when he did, she suddenly doubled over in pain as if she'd been punched in the gut and passed out on the floor. We pulled her up onto the bed, and she was okay a moment later, but the house suddenly erupted in a cacophony of activity.

A tri-field electromagnetic field detector we had set up in her bedroom near the primary source of disturbance started chirping its high-pitched squeal, and the back door to the master bedroom suddenly blew open. We closed the door only for it to blow open again seconds later. We closed it again and dead-bolted it while Carl conducted a blessing over the door.

We continued the cleansing of the house, with the distinct purpose of pushing it out into the backyard and beyond, off the property. While we were outside bearing crosses and candles, the wind kicked up into a gale, howling about us as the homeowner's cats circled the group in a frenzy. Somehow, the candles never blew out, and when we were done, the wind completely subsided, and Carl dropped to a knee.

The entity was gone, and the last time I talked to the family a couple years ago, it was still gone. Throughout the entire house cleansing I had been carrying a digital audio recorder mounted to me on an armband. When I later reviewed it, I was shocked at what I discovered. During the blessing Carl conducted in the master bedroom over the young woman, just before she doubled over in pain as if she'd been punched is the distinct voice of someone saying, "Die."

Can entities attach themselves to people?

MR: We've seen on many occasions that a spirit will attach itself to someone during an investigation and will follow that person home. This is quite different than a "possession" but similar to when an entity attaches itself to an object. Unfortunately, sometimes an entity will remain with a person and follow him or her around, creating an uncomfortable environment in which to live and work. There are spiritual cleansing measures we take in these cases to remove the attachment and send the spirit on its way.

Do you believe some people may be more susceptible to possession than others?

MR: People's energy vibrates at different levels, which I believe can attract entities of varying types. We see with psychic mediums that spirits are drawn to them as if they're beacons on that alternate plane of existence. The same is true, I believe, with all people in that their spiritual energy has a certain resonance, and that resonance is attractive to various others on the spiritual plane.

Are there any measures you take to protect yourself when you're in the field?

MR: I simply say a little prayer to myself when I enter and leave a location, and I believe that's enough. Some people perform small ceremonies before starting an investigation or arm themselves with small stones (I do too, on occasion), and I'm fine with all of that. I believe it comes down to faith. No matter the religion, talisman, stone, or artifact, if you believe in the depths of your soul that this thing, whatever it is, is going to protect you, then it will protect you.

How do you explain what's happening when a house is haunted? Is there science to back it up? What is your theory?

MR: This is, perhaps, the most difficult task for a paranormal investigator—proving it. During our investigations, we capture plenty of paranormal activity in the form of video, photographs, audio files, and device activations that appear to be a form of interaction and communication. Most investigators refer to this as "evidence."

Scores of paranormal investigative teams around the world state that they take a "scientific approach" to their investigations, but this usually amounts to them simply using an array of electronic gadgets and electing not to employ the services of a psychic medium. Personally, I prefer to use both.

In order to utilize the scientific method, investigators must perform a battery of tests on their hypotheses, make observations from those tests, and draw a conclusion. However, there is one prevailing problem for paranormal investigators using this method, and it comes during the testing phase: There is no constant. You can't make paranormal activity happen on demand. There is no related test in the paranormal field to dropping a feather in a vacuum and timing its descent again and again and again. One can sit in a room for days and observe absolutely nothing out of the ordinary, then give up, only to randomly spot an apparition in that room one fine afternoon, then sit right back in that room for days on end waiting for that apparition again to no avail.

As for my theory, spirits are people, but they don't have a physical body. As people they also have free will and the same emotional traits they had when they were alive. If someone was reclusive in life, it's likely they'll be reclusive in the afterlife, so trying to communicate with them may prove to be difficult. I believe in building a rapport with these spirits, just as I would build a rapport with any living person today. We don't barge into a living person's home, demand they turn on lights, open doors, or rap on the walls, and subject them to a game of Twenty Questions. I believe treating these nonliving people as people will help open the doors to discovering the secrets to the afterlife we've been seeking.

In your experience, have you noticed an increase or decrease in hauntings or paranormal occurrences?

MR: Many believe that there has been an increase in hauntings and paranormal activity of late, but this must be put into context. There was a period of time in our history in which stating you heard voices or saw Aunt Ethel who has been dead for ten years at the top of the stairs would earn you a trip to an insane asylum. At best, one may have been ridiculed or ostracized. Thus, many people kept quiet about their experiences, so we don't know how much legitimate paranormal activity was occurring because it wasn't being reported on a regular basis.

In today's age with so many television shows and movies now being dedicated to the experiences people have had with the paranormal, people have felt more comfortable coming forth and sharing. Now, everyone seems to be having paranormal experiences, and the difficulty for us lies in determining which are true and which are fabrications. We saw this during the Spiritualism movement in the 1800s as well, so it could be that our acceptance of these phenomena as a culture may be cyclical in nature.

CHAPTER 9

The Place Where
Evil Dwells

There are some places in the world, whether natural or man-made, that are known to be mysterious, haunted, hexed, or even possessed by evil forces. These physical locations or structures may have historical or archaeological evidence associated with them to indicate that horrific things occurred. In some cases, we are able to see the evidence of heinous activities of the past at these sites, such as disturbing mass graves or skeletons with missing bones or smashed skulls. Other places may only offer written accounts of grisly deeds or fiendish undertakings, leaving us to interpret the details and imagine the terrors that may have happened. Still other locales offer no such proof beyond legend or folklore that anything necessarily happened to curse them, but they just *feel* evil. What could make these places give off such an energy? Is it simply their macabre appearances?

Is it their backstories? Perhaps examining some places believed to hold negative energy will challenge your concept of evil and fear. The following is a fascinating assortment of places where evil is said to dwell.

Mayan Hell

Roughly 120 miles west/southwest of the vacation paradise of Cancún, near the center of the tip of Mexico's Yucatán Peninsula, lies an ancient gateway to the underworld. During the height of the pre-Columbian Mayan culture (approximately 250–950 CE), a series of mystical caves were revered as the entrance to Xibalba (pronounced *shee-Bal-ba,* meaning "place of fear"). The Mayans believed that when people died, their souls began a new journey to reach Tamoanchan, a place of eternal peace and beauty. The multistep journey was perilous and fraught with danger, beginning with the first nine steps through the dark abyss of Xibalba. Some of the sacred caves are a series of underground chambers linked by slippery footpaths embedded with gnarled tree roots and vines, their floors teeming with snakes, spiders, and scorpions creeping among the broken potsherds and skull fragments. Slick and uneven staircases lead into the darkness, some into underground lakes, others beneath a living canopy of groping roots and the leathery wings of roosting bats.

According to Mayan legends, the only way for souls to bypass this hellish portal on their voyages to paradise and avoid encountering the trickster Xibalbans was to die honorably, such as in warfare, as a sacrificial victim, on the ball court, or in childbirth. Ixtab, the Mayan goddess of suicide who appeared as a rotting corpse hanging by a noose, could also escort souls past the slashing stalactites and stalagmites projecting from both ceilings and floors in the "chamber of knives."

More than 450 years ago, Spanish explorers encountered the descendents of the Mayan people, no longer living as the thriving nation who built the sophisticated stone pyramids and temples in the jungle. Instead, the Mayans were a remnant culture of subsistence farmers living pastoral lifestyles. The Spaniards appointed bishop Diego de Landa in 1549 to identify heathen Mayans who failed to embrace Christ. Most Mayans accepted the notion of a resurrected deity rather easily because Christ's story was similar enough to their own maize god, but Landa believed that a secret sect of rebel Mayan heretics was growing, and he aimed to crush their movement. By 1562 the bishop had begun to implement cruel torture methods to root out the suspected heathens among the Mayans. The bishop discovered a Mayan temple at Mani and burned or destroyed more than forty sacred Mayan codices (books) in his efforts to free the people of "the Devil's trickery," but some remained intact and have since been discovered in Europe. These provide modern scholars with invaluable information about the Mayans.

Mexican archaeologists spent more than five years studying the codices, as well as the Inquisition trial records, which revealed the locations of places where the Mayans performed their pagan rituals. Using this data, the researchers were able to ask the local people to help them identify the locations of the Xibalba caves, which has added immensely to the mysteries of the Mayan culture and its many wonderful relics.

Transylvania's Mysterious Forest

In the middle of a primordial forest shrouded in milky blue-white fog, a near perfect oval exists where no trees grow. The empty ellipse, which can be clearly seen from the air, has had its soil laboratory tested. Science has been unable to determine why this barren patch of Earth has persisted throughout recorded history. Soil scientists have stated that there are no apparent reasons for this area to continue to defy nature. The Clearing, as it's often referred to, is considered the most terrifying place in what has been called the most terrifying forest in the world. The Clearing attracts Romanian witches and mediums who believe that the area is magical, perhaps a gate to another dimension, but only by the light of day. The forest is named Hoia Baciu, after a shepherd who went missing there with his entire flock of more than two hundred sheep. Few venture into the mystical wilderness by day; only the foolhardy dare to remain there overnight.

The forest is located in the Carpathian foothills near Cluj-Napoca, Romania's fourth-largest city and the unofficial capital of the Transylvania region. Hoia Baciu has been referred to as the Bermuda Triangle of Transylvania. Legends of this wild land speak of encounters with the Devil himself, along with demons, ghosts, and other spirits of the dead. A five-year-old girl who disappeared into the forest is purported to have reemerged five years later in the same clothes, having not aged a day. Another account suggests that a missing woman was found at the edge of the wood with a fifteenth-century coin in her pocket.

Many trees in the area are twisted into strange shapes, including zigzags and exaggerated S-curves at the bases of some their trunks, and trees that have grown together to form sweeping arcs and ovate frames. Some branches are braided together like thick strands of living rope. Unlike most temperate forests, Hoia Baciu is mostly silent; the chorus of insects and birdsong is noticeably absent. Visitors claim that the eerie silence is interrupted only by whispers that seem to emanate from their own minds. Even esteemed professors at Babeş-Bolyai University in nearby Cluj-Napoca will admit that they believe this damned forest may be haunted.

A Romanian military technician named Emil Barnea captured what he claimed were images of a UFO hovering over the Clearing in 1968. The Communist government at that time had no tolerance for esoteric or paranormal beliefs within its citizenry, and especially so for military personnel. Barnea had everything to lose by reporting his photos and sightings, and he was subsequently removed from his post, leading UFO investigators to argue that Barnea's images should be considered among the most credible accounts due to the risks to his career and freedom he took to produce them.

Shadowy figures and other strange phenomena still haunt the forest. Visitors report feelings of being watched, along with anxiety, nausea, headaches, and mysterious burns and skin abrasions. Failure of electronic devices regularly occurs in the forest, especially near the Clearing. Images captured on cameras are sometimes not in the same order as they were taken. Other instruments have measured anomalies and bizarre fluctuations in the electromagnetic field and infrasound recording devices have picked up puzzling echoes. Some have claimed to have seen ghostly men through the trees dressed in traditional Romanian garb from centuries ago. Others allege they walked by certain twisted trees and discovered that hours had passed in what seemed like minutes.

Ireland's Haunted Castle

Leap Castle (pronounced *Lep*) has been the site of vicious carnage and grisly murders over its more than eight-hundred-year history. It is no wonder then that this craggy Gothic structure is considered by many to be one of the most haunted relics of old Europe. Its precise construction date is unknown. Some experts believe that it was built sometime in the twelfth century, and others claim that it was considerably later, in the fifteenth century.

The castle was known to have been constructed over a site that was previously used by Celtic druids to perform pagan ceremonies. It was originally named Leim Ui Bhanain, meaning "Leap of the O'Bannons," a moniker that describes the circumstances of sibling rivals of the O'Bannon clan and their claim over the land. Legend has it that two brothers were in a dispute to determine who would lead the clan and the castle's construction, so they challenged one another to leap from a high rock nearby. The survivor would reign as the new clan chieftain.

The O'Bannons built the castle, then lost it shortly thereafter to the rival O'Carroll clan in a violent takeover. The O'Carrolls fought to maintain their rule of the castle, twice fending off seizure attempts by the Earl of Kildar. The passing centuries of O'Carroll control of the castle were marked by fearsome acts of violence as clan members jockeyed for leadership. In one shocking encounter, a dispute over succession to lead the clan ended in 1532 when Teige O'Carroll stormed into the main hall and drove his sword into the back of his older brother Thaddeus, a priest, as he was performing mass. Thaddeus died on the altar in front of the mortified family, thus continuing a legacy of brutality and murder. The apparition of the priest is said to be just one of many specters that have haunted the Gothic stronghold over its history.

Leap Castle front, County Offaly, Ireland.

Other ghosts that have been seen in the castle are said to be members of the McMahon family. The O'Carrolls held a feast in their honor to celebrate the McMahons' victory over a mutual rival clan, but the festivity turned out to be an evil ruse. The McMahons were served poisoned food, and all members of their clan perished as their hosts looked on.

The wicked O'Carrolls were known to have used the castle itself as a weapon. In the northeastern corner of the structure, workmen in 1922 discovered a secret oubliette, a sinister hole-like dungeon that can only be entered through a trapdoor in the floor above. The word "oubliette" comes from Middle French *oulbier*, "to forget." Unsuspecting guests would have been guided to stand over the trap, then dropped into the pit below. Their victims' screams likely entertained others in the hall as they were left to die, impaled on large, inverted wooden spikes. The workmen removed enough human skeletons to fill a large cart three times.

Another frightening spirit said to roam the grounds is that of the Red Lady. Her form is described as a tall woman draped in a scarlet gown who holds a dagger and is surrounded by a glowing mist. Witnesses say that rooms become intensely cold whenever this wraith appears. Legends say that this was once a beautiful woman who was captured by men of the O'Carroll clan and held against her will in the castle, where she was tortured and raped repeatedly. She bore an infant as a result of these atrocities, who was then murdered by her captors. It is said that the new mother was so distraught by her ordeal that as soon as she was left unattended, she found a dagger and killed herself. Sightings of this ghost are usually accompanied by the chilling sounds of her mournful sobs.

Ownership of Leap Castle was finally passed to the Darby family through marriage in 1659. Generations of the Darby family learned to coexist with various paranormal entities for centuries. A Darby ancestor is credited with unleashing the most horrifying phantom at the castle. The Elemental is believed by some to have been a protective spirit conjured by the druids who lived there before the castle was built to keep the site sacred for their magic rites. Other myths contend that the Elemental is a ghost of an O'Carroll clansman who died from leprosy, which might explain its hideous appearance with a decomposing face and revolting stench.

Mildred Darby was a dark gothic novelist who dabbled in the occult. She regularly conducted séances at the castle in the early

1900s, and it was at one of these sessions that she apparently awakened the vile spirit, which she described as inhuman, with eyes like black cavities and the stench of a decomposing corpse.

The Darbys were an English family and abandoned the castle in 1922 during the time Ireland was fighting for independence from Great Britain. While they were in exile, the Irish Republican Army bombed and looted the castle during its revolt. Leap Castle was dormant for more than fifty years after that, until it was purchased in the 1970s by Australian historian Peter Bartlett, himself the progeny of the original O'Bannon clan. He claimed to have witnessed a great number of paranormal events before his death in 1989, and even hired a "white witch" to cleanse the castle of its malevolent spirits. The castle was purchased in 1991 by musician Sean Ryan and his wife, Anne, who have continued to restore the haunted castle.

The Danish Lady in White

In approximately 1215, Peder Sunesen, bishop of Roskilde, began construction of a fortified medieval palace between meadows and a lake on the small island of Zealand, near an isthmus in present-day Denmark. The castle was named Dragsholm, which means "the islet by the drag"; *drag* refers to the isthmus. The structure was the only castle known to survive the Count's Feud, Denmark's civil war that raged from 1534 to 1536. Also called the Count's War, this period of violence brought about the Protestant Reformation in Denmark. In the ensuing years, Catholicism was outlawed, and the castle served as a prison until about 1564, housing bishops and other Catholic clergy, along with other former noblemen from the area.

One of the prison's inmates was James Hepburn, the fourth Earl of Bothwell and third husband to Mary, Queen of Scots. Hepburn was wanted by the English Crown for allegedly murdering Mary's second husband. He left Scotland and sought refuge abroad, but a strong North Sea storm knocked his ship off-course, sending him to Bergen, Norway. At that time, Norway was under Danish rule, and Hepburn was captured and charged with holding incorrect papers. He had earlier been engaged to Anna Throndsen, whom he abandoned after convincing her to sell most of her possessions. He also swindled her parents into giving him vast sums of money so that he could leave Norway to pursue a life among the French elites, where he made his way into the royal court.

This social butterfly was brought to justice and the Danish king sent him to Dragsholm, where he was chained to a pillar. He spent nearly ten years pacing around the pillar until his death in April of 1578. He went insane during his captivity, wearing a circular groove in the floor of his cell that can still be seen today. People have reported hearing chains and shuffling footsteps when all is quiet.

Dragsholm remained a prison until sometime between 1658 and 1660 when King Charles X Gustav of Sweden attacked it during the Dano-Swedish War. The heavily damaged structure was abandoned and left derelict until it was ceded by the king to grocer Heinrich Müller to settle outstanding debts. Müller began the process of restoring the castle, but with the baroque embellishments that we can see today.

Sometime in the early 1700s, some of the most heinous acts are said to have been committed by a nobleman who lived in the castle, possibly Frederik Christian Adeler, the former governor of Rockilde. A legend persists that tells of an aristocratic young lady who lived in the castle, the daughter of a nobleman who was betrothed to marry the son of another elite family. Although she knew that it would have been completely unacceptable for her to fall in love with someone of her choosing, she did, in fact, follow her heart and strike up a romantic relationship with a commoner who worked on the castle grounds. She tried to keep her feelings hidden, but her father was aware of her fascination with the young man. The landlord tolerated his daughter's affections with little regard until it became obvious that her love affair had resulted in her becoming noticeably pregnant. The father then held a special dinner for his daughter to celebrate her upcoming marriage, but secretly poisoned her food with some type of tranquilizer. She must have awakened in darkness to discover that she had been sentenced to death by her own father as punishment for her disgrace, trapped in the claustrophobic hell of a sealed tomb between castle walls. She was bricked up into a space just slightly larger than her body, from where castle laborers could hear her muffled cries and scratches for some time until she finally fell silent.

Her tortured soul is said to be seen and heard in the castle, mournfully wailing in her spectral white gown. Shortly after World War I, workmen were removing ancient castle bricks as part of a renovation project and made a macabre discovery. Beneath dust and broken fragments of brick and mortar, the men uncovered a centuries-old skeleton sheathed in a tattered white gown.

Crypts of Bones

The Ordo Fratrum Minorum Capuccinorum (Order of Friars Minor Capuchin) was a movement of Franciscan monks in Rome whose brothers devoted themselves to practicing the humble ways of Francis, their patron saint. The reformist sect was established in the 1520s, and despite the hostility and threats that the Order faced, it eventually thrived with the financial support of some of Rome's wealthiest families nearly a century later. The Capuchin friary relocated to the Santa Maria della Concezione in 1631. The Capuchins—so named for the *capuche,* or hood on their habit—were ordered by the noble brother of Pope Urban VIII to gather the remains of all deceased members of their sect and move them to their new home. For reasons lost to history, the monks began to decorate the five rooms of the subterranean crypt beneath the small church with the bones of their disinterred brothers. Today, the Capuchin Crypt is a disturbingly beautiful ossuary that features the decorative arrangement of skeletal parts of nearly four thousand people, including Capuchin friars as well as indigent Romans and orphans.

A ghastly, yet intriguing place, the Capuchin Crypt is an exhibition of the bizarre. By order of the pope, deceased friars were buried without caskets in soil brought from Jerusalem. As more monks died, the longest-buried corpses were exhumed, their bodies having typically spent decades decomposing in the holy earth. Their bones were then cleaned and used to make elaborate adornments and arrangements, such as grim chandeliers and candelabras, rosettes, crosses, crowns, and coats of arms. Some mummified monks dressed in dusty habits with braided rope closures still feature bits of darkened, leathery skin clinging to bones. The five ossuary rooms of the crypt have been given apt names related to the bulk of the types of bones on display, such as the Crypt of Skulls, the Crypt of the Leg Bones and Thigh Bones, and the Crypt of the Pelvises.

By the 1870s, Roman authorities had criminalized the display of human remains, forcing the Order to cease its strange commemoration of the dead. By then, the ossuary had reached a level of renown that attracted the attentions of the morbidly curious. The Capuchins believe that the crypt should be available for others to visit and quietly contemplate the value of life and to consider that death may come at any time; thus, the location has been somewhat of a tourist destination for more than a hundred years. A plaque at the entrance states: "What you are now, we once were; what we are now, you shall be."

Ossuaries are any space, from a small container to a large, open cavern or catacomb, that contains human skeletal remains. Ossuaries have a long history and are surprisingly more common than most would think. Chambered tombs filled with the bones of the dead were used in prehistoric times and persisted through the ages into the modern era. Often, ossuaries served practical purposes, acting as mass graves for thousands during times of overwhelming circumstances, such as war, plagues, famine, or natural disasters. Other ossuaries, such as the Capuchin Crypt, are the result of special funerary practices where space is limited.

Perhaps the largest and most frightening ossuary is the famous underground caverns of the Catacombs of Paris (French: *Catacombes de Paris*). The catacombs are an extensive series of tunnels situated more than sixty feet (approximately twenty meters) beneath the city that stretch for hundreds of miles. The centuries-old tunnels were remnants of ancient limestone deposits that were mined to provide the necessary materials to build the city. By the 1600s, Parisian cemeteries were overflowing with the corpses of every person who had lived and died there. Cemeteries often exuded the noxious stench of decomposing flesh, and by 1780, a period of heavy spring rains caused a retaining wall around Les Innocents, the city's oldest and largest cemetery, to collapse and spill rotting corpses into the streets. A solution was needed, and by 1786, a plan to exhume between six million and seven million human remains and move them into the city's former quarries was underway; an enormous civic project that took more than twelve years to complete and actually continued through the French Revolution and subsequent Reign of Terror.

Another famous European ossuary is located in Sedlec in the Czech Republic. The Sedlec Ossuary is beneath the Cemetery Church of All Saints and believed to contain the skeletons of nearly seventy thousand people. Many thousands of people were lost during the Black Death in the fourteenth century, leaving the small Gothic abbey church and mausoleum overwhelmed. As at other overburdened cemeteries, the monks who oversaw Sedlec determined that the best solution was to exhume the dead-and-buried and stack the bones within the chapel. In the early eighteenth century, renovations to the chapel took place in order to repair and preserve the structure. The work was designed in the baroque style. A talented woodcarver named František Rint was employed by the Schwarzenberg family in 1870 to organize the heap of thousands of bones. The creative artisan appeared to have been inspired by baroque ornate detail and proceeded to use the abundance of human bones to sculpt and produce the Schwarzenberg family crest, as well as chandeliers, garlands, and other morbid decorations.

Human bones make up the Schwarzenberg coat of arms
in the Sedlec Ossuary, Kutná Hora, Czech Republic.

Whether one finds them evil, gruesome, strangely appealing, or spiritually moving, ossuaries have existed and endured in both the Old and the New World since the Zoroastrians first built them more than three thousand years ago in Persia. The highest concentration of ossuaries remains in Europe, standing primarily as solutions for areas lacking sufficient burial space. Many of the larger European ossuaries, including the Capuchin Crypt and the Catacombs of Paris, operate today as museums and are open to the public.

Bavarian Haunted Convent

Belief in the dark arts, witchcraft, and demonic possession persisted well into the Age of Enlightenment in parts of rural Germany longer than in other areas of Europe. One case involved the eventual possession of a group of ten Norbertine nuns in the cloistered convent of Unterzell, near Würzburg. Beginning in 1744, the nuns spoke of hearing mysterious growls, moans, and other bestial sounds, seeing shadowy figures within the walls of the monastery, and witnessing the phantom movements of large pieces of furniture. Over the course of the next three years, a series of intermittent exorcisms occurred with varied results as some of the nuns appeared to be plagued by demonic forces. Maria Renata Sänger von Mossau, the sixty-nine-year-old subprioress of the nunnery was eventually convicted of bewitching the other sisters and sending demons to possess them.

Renata Sänger came from a family of lower nobility and was forced into the cloister in 1699, when she was nineteen. After serving the monastery faithfully for fifty years, Sister Maria opposed the acceptance of Cecilia Pistorini as a nun in 1745 due to Pistorini's displays of unusual behavior, including convulsions, hallucinations, and delusions. Pistorini was confirmed as a nun, regardless of Renata Sänger's objections. In 1749, another nun began to suffer from hearing strange voices, chronic headaches, and fainting. Soon afterward, more nuns exhibited similar symptoms. The bizarre behaviors increased and included actions that were deemed to have been unmistakable signs of demonic possession: screaming during recitals of the Divine Office, painful and debilitating seizures, inconsolable writhing and moaning, and even foaming at the mouth. When one of the accursed sisters was succumbing to her madness and on her deathbed, she accused Sister Maria of bewitching her. Word of this implication spread beyond the walls of the convent and reached the ear of Father Oswald Loschert of the Oberzell monastery, which led to an investigation. The bishop of Würzburg presided over the inquest.

The accused was interrogated and ultimately tortured, and finally relented. Under great duress, Maria Renata Sänger von Mossau confessed to heresy, admitted that she was a practicing witch and guilty of bewitching others. She described having signed a pact with the Devil as a child with her own blood and said she had sworn herself to Satan at age seven. By age twelve, she claimed to have been baptized at a black mass before becoming a child prostitute. Renata Sänger went on to testify that she used dark magic to create and release diseased vermin such as rats and insects, that she desecrated the Host, and that she regularly engaged in intercourse with Satan and his minions. The bishop accepted these admissions at face value and presented her case to the impassioned judges of the local civil court. Renata Sänger was convicted, and while she was imprisoned, the remaining nuns who seemed possessed were thoroughly exorcised. Her room was swept, and her collection of poisons, ointments, and potions were discovered. The heretical nun's verdict was announced on June 18, 1749. Three days after receiving the sacrament of penance, she was publicly beheaded, and her body was burned. Her head was then displayed on a spike for all to see.

The news of the Unterzell case outraged Pope Benedict XIV. The pope censured the bishop for his unenlightened beliefs and compared the killing of an elderly nun to the scandal of the infamous Spanish Inquisition. Although the original Unterzell Monastery was destroyed to its foundation during World War II, it is said that nearly three hundred years after her death, the hostile spirit of Sister Maria can still be felt, and sometimes seen, haunting the grounds near its former site in Würzburg.

The Sanatorium of the White Death

As the afternoon sun dipped and the shadows grew longer across the swampy bottomlands less than a mile from the Ohio River, a former Churchill Downs groom leaned forward and continued to cough relentlessly. He was in his final days, and he suffered the curse of knowledge that his end was near. He no longer spent mornings convalescing on the open-air sundeck. Every miserable day had become excruciating since the surgeries to remove two pairs of his lower ribs. The sutures above his diaphragm had never fully healed, and they often cracked and leaked during violent coughing fits. On days like these, the forty-one-year-old father to three simply sat in a wheeled chair, facing a dull gray-green wall so that he would not have to watch others with his condition endure his same fate. Every evening, he wished for the hands of eternal darkness to smother him so that he could escape his affliction. The former stable hand and caretaker of thoroughbreds suffered the ravages of the White Death, as many in his family had before him. Once again, he wiped his forehead and eyes with his sweat-soaked handkerchief, blindly depositing wet spurts of blood and sputum from his previous bout of coughing.

The man soon died, and his body was abruptly wheeled away, carted down a hidden corridor known as the body chute in a futile effort to mitigate the gloom of despair at the Waverly Hills Sanatorium, the final home for nearly all of those stricken with tuberculosis in northwest Kentucky in the early part of the twentieth century. Kentucky was particularly hard hit with the disease, often referred to then as "consumption" due to the ways in which the disease consumed its victims. More Kentuckians died of tuberculosis during the fifty-six months of World War II than those who died in battle from wounds or disease combined. Prior to the 1943 breakthrough discovery of the antibiotic streptomycin as an effective treatment, consumption was a leading cause of death. The disease's high rate of mortality made the body chute at Waverly Hills Sanatorium a busy passageway to nearby railroad tracks where bodies were loaded onto waiting train cars.

Up to sixty-three thousand people may have died there during its forty-nine-year existence. With improved tuberculosis treatments, the need for the sanatorium was gradually reduced until the facility closed for good in 1961. It was reopened the following year as the Woodhaven Geriatric Sanatorium, an extended-care hospital that treated aging patients with various forms of mental illness and dementia. The state closed the facility in 1982 after twenty years of reports of horrible conditions and claims of patient abuses, including unusual experiments and electroshock treatments.

Ownership of the building has changed hands a number of times in the decades since the sanatorium was forced to close. Waverly Hills stood derelict for years since the turn of the millennium, attracting the homeless, vandals, and thrill seekers. The institution gained a reputation as an epicenter of paranormal activity. With all of the pain, suffering, death, and despair that occurred in the building, it is now considered one of the most haunted places in the United States. Many legends have emerged, with regard to spectral sights and sounds of tortured souls, some of which are said to feel benign, whereas others may look or sound menacing. Ghost hunters and paranormal investigators have reported hearing phantasmal sounds including creaks, moans, drips, footsteps, doors closing, furniture moving, and eerie voices.

Phantom smells have also been described, including those of cooked foods and freshly baked bread. Spectral lights and spirits have been witnessed on all floors, but many fantastic legends concerning the horrors of the fifth floor persist. An account from 1928 describes the hanging death of the head nurse in Room 502. She was said to have been approximately twenty-nine years old, purportedly unwed and with child. No one can say how long she may have been suspended from the room's light fixture before her body was found.

Another tragedy involving a nurse who worked in Room 502 is said to have happened just four years later, in 1932. This young woman's broken body was supposedly found several stories below the rooftop patio.

The most ominous presence reported at Waverly Hills is known as the Creeper. Some believe that it is a terrifying, demonic being that seems to crawl along floors and walls like a dreadful, living shadow. Witnesses say that seeing the Creeper immediately fills you with the overwhelming feelings of pain and anguish of the thousands of souls who suffered there. At least one account indicates that the Creeper was capable of blocking the beam of a flashlight shining between two witnesses. Both were left terrorized and subsequently mired in feelings of doom and despair.

The Haunted Superliner

On her maiden transatlantic voyage, the *RMS Queen Mary* became the flagship superliner of the Cunard-White Star Line and was recognized as being the fastest ship to cross from Southampton, England, to New York City later that year. During her storied years of service from 1936 to 1967, the *Queen Mary* moved more than two million passengers across the North Atlantic, as well as nearly nine hundred thousand allied troops after she was retrofitted into one of the fastest personnel transport vessels for the duration of World War II. The ship was officially retired after departing Southampton on Halloween, 1967, when she sailed to her final home in the port of Long Beach, California. There she remains permanently moored and continues to serve as a major tourist attraction that features a museum and hotel with restaurants and specialty tours

There were forty-nine recorded deaths aboard the *Queen Mary* throughout her active years. She was painted in a series of grays from the Royal Navy's palette when she served as a wartime troop transport and nicknamed the *Grey Ghost,* an ironic moniker given the many tales of her supernatural phenomena. Guests of the ship have reported creepy experiences both during her active years and her years in Long Beach. Visitors have shared accounts of seeing mysterious orbs and hearing knocks, bangs, screams, door slams, and the sounds of crying children. Paranormal investigators believe that there may be as many as 150 spirits and entities roaming the ship's decks and cavernous boiler rooms. To this day, employees and contractors on board prefer to work in pairs rather than to be found alone, even during the daytime.

Investigators have compiled their evidence and identified some of the more common spectral entities said to be perceived on the ship. One such specter is known as Amanda, a name heard through EVP (electronic voice phenomenon) recording devices. This calm female spirit can be heard talking and singing inside the boiler rooms. She appears to be drawn more to women.

Another presence felt in the boiler rooms is known to be less tolerant toward women. Paranormal investigators have researched the ship's logs and feel that this may be the ghost of a former boiler-room worker named John Henry who was killed while on the job.

Some have claimed to see the ethereal apparition of British prime minister Winston Churchill, sometimes even accompanied by the smell of cigar smoke. Churchill reserved the entire M Deck at certain points during the Second World War, from which he planned the D-Day invasion. Guests have also reported seeing groups of spectral men in World War II military attire.

The Lady in White is perhaps the most frequently sighted spirit, often spotted near the A Deck lobby. Many believe that her floating apparitional form and white appearance are a reflection of her role as a former nurse on the ship. Visitors have also reported hearing the tragic splashing of five- or six-year-old Jaqueline Torin, who drowned in a pool that is now occupied by the Royal Theater. Ghost hunters using EVP equipment claim to capture "Little Jackie's" last gasps.

The *Queen Mary* has been featured on numerous paranormal investigation television programs and was named number six among the world's top ten most haunted spaces by *TIME Magazine* in 2008. The ship's operators and investors have hoped to capitalize on the lore of her haunted past by hosting ghost tours, Halloween events, and overnight stays in their guest suites that are notorious for paranormal activity. In response to relentless requests, the ship's room B340, which had been sealed off from public use for more than forty years, was recently opened and renovated for guests. According to the ship's logs, passengers and staff have witnessed flickering lights, mysterious sounds, the faucet turning on and off, and doors opening and closing by themselves. Visitors are now able to book the room with access to a large chest stocked with ghost-hunting equipment, a Ouija board, tarot cards, crystals, and other mediums for contacting the spirit world.

CHAPTER 10

The Most Horrific Archaeological Finds

As an archaeologist, working in the field may include long days of monotonous sifting, or worse yet, surveying. However, there are some days that you encounter things that are so horrific that you wish you could go back to the lab and just scrub some potsherds. Some of these discoveries could convince even the most ardent skeptic that evil does exist and perhaps demons too. Nevertheless, the ability to remain objective is the charge of the modern researcher, so even the most gruesome discoveries have their place in the human experience, even if they are difficult to fathom.

Neolithic Massacre

A team of European archaeologists has started the excavation of a massive bone pit, the latest in a series of Stone Age discoveries that reveal gruesome evidence of carnivorous feasts. The naked bones show traces of scratches and scrape marks consistent with meat removal; some bones are charred and others, such as vertebrae and long bones, fractured so that prehistoric human fingers could have probed their insides to extract nutrionally dense marrow. The mass grave from more than seven thousand years ago uncovered near present-day Herxheim, Germany, has confirmed what many archaeologists have long suspected. It appears that Neolithic farmers in central Europe were likely to have engaged in regular acts of systematic violence—and cannibalism.

The site has revealed the expertly butchered bones of at least five hundred humans, and researchers believe that number could easily end up being twice that when more of the site is further excavated. DNA analysis of some of the remains shows that the victims were migrants from other areas of Europe, some from as far away as present-day northwest France.

I believe that some religious elements drove these people to undertake arduous walking journeys of many hundreds of miles to this tiny hamlet as part of some type of ritualistic pilgrimage. Many theories exist about just who the dead were, but so far, no evidence has been discovered to solve the mysteries of how so many nonnative people could have ended up on the menu of a small Stone Age village. Some of my colleagues have proposed that the victims were not eaten after all, but were simply stripped of their flesh as part of a vicious ritual, but I see the evidence differently. That idea seems just as preposterous as my hypothesis, which considers that the human bones bore the same marks as those found on butchered livestock. None of the bones showed signs of malnutrition, poor health, or wounds from battle. Some bone fragments were from infants, stillborn babies, and even unborn fetuses, and the majority of others were from older children, women, and some men. Marks on many of the bones seem to indicate that flesh was flame charred on skewers. Carbon dating shows that the village only lasted approximately fifty years before it either collapsed or was abandoned. It appears to me that this site may have been a small village populated by a powerful group of shamans or warriors who exacted a heavy toll of volunteer human sacrifices.

Pits of Severed Hands

Austrian archaeologists working in the hot Egyptian sun near Tel el-Daba, the present site of the ancient city of Avaris, recently discovered two severed right hands in shallow pits. The grisly find confirmed the validity of hieroglyphs and biblical verses that depict warriors cutting off the hands of their vanquished opponents. Egyptian lore describes the practice as proof of an enemy's defeat, with the severed hands exchanged like bounties for gold.

Two more pits have since been discovered in this part of the Nile Delta, northeast of Cairo, that contain an additional fourteen severed hands—all of them right hands. It is believed that severing the hands of conquered enemies was considered an act of valor, as well as a symbolic punishment by depriving them of power in the afterlife.

Alken Enge Slaughter

Around the time of Christ, an army of nearly 400 Germanic barbarians were gravely defeated in battle by a mysterious and powerful adversary. The mutilated remains of men, mostly aged between thirteen and forty years, were discovered well preserved in a sprawling peat bog near Alken Enge, on the shore of Lake Mossø on Denmark's Jutland Peninsula. In 2012, archaeologists began to remove and catalog the adult male bodies and parts, and they've been able to determine that this carnage likely occurred in a single day of savage warfare.

Roman accounts of the wild barbarians of Germania offer us little detail about the sizes of their tribes. The Roman Empire's northern frontier was nearly two hundred miles south of the Danish lake-turned-bog where the remains were discovered, so we could reasonably assume that the vanquished were likely defeated by a rival Iron Age Germanic tribe.

The bones that have so far been recovered paint a picture of tribal brutality that defies imagination. Traumatic injuries and mortal wounds such as missing limbs and crushed skulls were the result of heavy blows from swords, axes, maces, and other weapons.

Researchers from Skanderborg Museum, Moesgård Museum, and Aarhus University studying the remains in attempts to better understand the sequence of events that led to the bloodshed have made an important breakthrough. Based on their findings, it appears that the battle scene may have been revisited by the victors some time later. Animal gnaw marks on exposed bones suggest that the bodies may have remained on the battlefield for as long as six months before being collected and ritualistically cast into the waters of a nearby lake, which eventually became a bog. Whatever flesh that might have been left on the bone was removed. In one instance, four pelvic bones were found threaded onto a large stick for reasons unknown. Slaughtered animal remains and clay pots were also discovered in the peat, leading researchers to believe that secondary event may have been a sacred pagan ritual to honor the fallen.

Bog Bodies

In the peat bogs of Europe, archaeologists have found well-preserved victims of human sacrifices. Bog bodies are well preserved because of the acidity of the peat that covers them. Peat is a type of soil that is formed as a result of dead plants layering on top of each other, creating peat moss. The soil becomes acidic as a result, so the bodies of the people in the peat are preserved. The bones, the leathery skin, the teeth, the hair, and the clothes that remain on these bog bodies are all conserved to varying degrees. According to Roman historians, the Celts sometimes sacrificed people to beg for fertility for the land and cattle. The Germans brought human sacrifices to the war god Odin, and in Sweden, people were offered as human sacrifices until as late as the eleventh century.

In 1897, two workers who were out illegally burning peat discovered a human body in the Stijfveen peat bog near the village of Yde, Netherlands. This eerily well-preserved bog body terrified the men, who feared they might have unearthed a devil, but this was no demon. This was a teenage girl who had been in that bog for almost two thousand years. She was found with a half-shaved head and a rope around her neck. The news about the body quickly spread. The mayor of nearby Vries reported the discovery to the Provincial Museum in Assen. He described the body as having blue skin with damage to the right cheek, an open mouth, visible teeth, and long reddish hair on the left of the skull with the right side being clean shaven (Menotti and O'Sullivan, 2013).

Known as the Yde Girl, archaeologists later determined that parts of her body and clothing had been dug up by villagers; nearly all her teeth were stolen, and her hair was pulled loose. In life, the girl was strangled, as revealed by a woolen band with a slide button around her neck. A cut above her left collarbone indicated she was also stabbed with a knife. Research showed that the girl was sixteen when she died (sometime between 54 BCE and 128 CE). She had a spine abnormality that would have caused her to limp. This could also have meant that she was singled out in her community because of this defect.

In the mid-nineties, the University of Manchester along with a forensic artist reconstructed the Yde Girl's face in striking detail. The reconstruction shows us what this poor girl could have looked like and brings her back to life with astonishing realism. The Yde Girl had strawberry-blond hair, blue eyes, and slightly tanned skin according to this study. By making her seem real, the thought of her being sacrificed is that much more horrible.

Saint Brice's Day Massacre

On Friday, November 13, 1002, the Saxon king Æthelred the Unready, or the Ill-Advised, decreed that all Danes (people of Viking descent) living in England should be exterminated. The name of the massacre refers to Saint Brice, a fifth-century bishop whose feast day happened to have been held on the November 13. Æthelred, who had been king since he turned twelve, when his mother ordered the murder of his older step-brother, was viewed as an unstable and inept leader who was often prone to making foolish decisions. The king was told of a Danish assassination plot against him, which prompted his extermination charter. England had been subjected to Danish raids and occupation every year since the early 900s, and Saxon tension was building.

In the spring of 1002, he was married to the Norman Duke Richard's daughter, Emma, an act that bolstered his alliances with the Norman gentry and royalty and granted him the confidence to wage war upon the Danes. His decree had been issued on the advice of his leading advisors, but it was poorly organized and executed, which led only to cruel, sporadic killings in limited areas.

One of the more horrific Danish exterminations took place in Oxford. The event involved a group of threatened Danish families rushing into Saint Frideswide's church to seek sanctuary from roving hordes of English loyalists. The Danes presumed that they would be safe within the confines of the church, but the angry mob opted to burn the church down with the cowering Danes inside.

An even more ruthless extermination event apparently happened on the grounds of Oxford that day. In 2008, at least thirty-five battered and broken male skeletons were discovered on the grounds of Oxford's Saint John's College in an apparent mass grave. Archaeologists from the Thames Valley Archaeological Services discovered the remains during a survey before new construction began at the University of Oxford. Analysis of the bones indicates that they were all young men of Norwegian descent, which suggests that they may have been first- or second-generation Vikings. Radiocarbon dating of the bodies narrowed the range to 960–1020, which provided compelling evidence that these men were victims of the Saint Brice's Day Massacre.

What was most disturbing—and perhaps evil—was the forensic evidence that demonstrated the heinous ways in which these men perished. Skull injuries appeared to be mostly blade and puncture wounds to the backs of the men's heads that would have been more than sufficient to cause mortal fractures and brain injury. It was noted that typical injuries resulting from hand-to-hand combat with swords and other metal weapons often include gouges and fractures to the bones of the forearms due to the victims' final attempts to defend themselves with raised arms. None of those bone injuries are present with these skeletons. Nearly all of the damage was sustained from behind, suggesting that the Danes were just trying to flee for their lives.

The Saint Brice's Day Massacre was ultimately regarded as another in a line of strategic failures for King Æthelred. The actions led to vicious reprisals and increased Viking raids. After Æthelred's death in 1016, Cnut the Great, leader of the Danes, assumed the throne of all of England and took Emma of Normandy as his wife.

Medieval Ethnic Cleansing

In 2004, special investigators were called in to review newly discovered evidence related to a long-dead cold case involving the murders of seventeen individuals, eleven of them children and one just two years old. The evidence was discovered during the excavation phase of a major construction project in Norwich, a city in East Anglia, approximately one hundred miles northeast of London. Building progress at the Chapelfield Shopping Centre was delayed as archaeologists carefully unpacked the crime scene, removing seventeen skeletons from an ancient cavity that appeared to have been a medieval well. No other crime scene quite like this had ever been discovered in Britain before.

As the investigation continued, the research team grew to include anthropologists and forensic experts. The team employed the latest forensic techniques combined with traditional detective procedures using a mix of historical records, carbon dating, and isotopic bone analysis. Mitochondrial DNA samples were examined and the team was able to reach back to the twelfth or thirteenth century to effectively match and identify the victims, and the picture became clearer.

All of the data pointed to an ethnic cleansing. The most likely scenario was that a single extended Jewish family with European roots was the victim of a pogrom, an organized mass murder of a particular ethnic group. This Russian term generally applies to the cleansing of Jews in Russia or Eastern Europe. The sequence of events that led to this horrific tragedy may have involved accusations of crimes made by Christians against Jews. The historical record shows that the town of Norwich was home to a community of Jewish immigrants since the twelfth century. It also shows that as Christendom spread across England, a sense of scorn and mistrust against Jews worsened. That period saw a rise in mob violence against Jews that ultimately led to an era of expulsion. Records indicate that resentment and hostility grew against the Jewish community during the 1100s due to Christian beliefs that the Jews killed Jesus. Christians also generally loathed the Jews due to the perception of their focus on acquiring wealth. In 1190, a Norwich mob massacred large numbers of the town's Jewish people, possibly due to rumors that Jews had kidnapped and performed ritual killings of Christian children.

The bodies in the well appeared to have been thrown in, headfirst, beginning with the adults. The adult bones sustained fractures and traumatic damage due to the force of hitting the bottom of the well. The children's bones were spared much of this damage because the adult bodies cushioned their falls. The immediate survivors—some of the children and possibly an adult or two near the top of the heap—must have endured an agonizing hell on Earth for the few days they may have lived beyond those who died on impact below them. Perhaps they were taunted, spat upon, and cursed by their former neighbors who peered at them from above. Perhaps they were simply isolated in the bottom of the shaft, with no hope for escape or rescue.

Witch Bottles and Smoked Cats

One type of horrific find that archaeologists uncover more often than you might expect is the witch bottle. The practice of making witch bottles and burying them as a charm to ward off evil originated in England in the late Middle Ages but continued well into the twentieth century both in England and the United States (Manning, 2014). There were many different reasons people used witch bottles, but the one most often cited is bewitchment. These bottles were not like the ones used to trap jinn; that would not be horrific. Instead, these bottles contained urine and other bodily fluids mixed with insects, pins, and sharp objects that were meant to magically injure the witch and make it too painful for her to urinate. It was an oddly specific way to punish a witch.

In addition to punishing the witch, by burying a witch bottle at you home, you could prevent an evil witch attack or curse. In 2014, an archaeologist unearthed a beautifully preserved glass witch bottle in Newark-on-Trent in the United Kingdom. The six-inch-tall green bottle was buried at a building complex known as the Old Magnus Buildings to protect the area from evil spirits and witches. The bottle dated to around 1680. Historical evidence suggests most witch bottles used a similar recipe, but in England, some witch bottles were a little different. Some of the materials found in English witch bottles include leather hearts pierced with needles, human hair, fingernail clippings, sulfur, tallow, bone, pages from books, and written spells. Sometimes, English witch bottles are found with unidentified liquids that have remained unidentified because they have not undergone a chemical analysis. Witch bottles can be found in old homes and buildings behind walls, around chimneys, and under floorboards. If you have a very old home, you could have one buried somewhere, especially if you live in New England. Lucky you!

Possibly for similar reasons, cats described as "smoked" have been found buried around homes. The gruesome and sad practice is thought to be even older than burying witch bottles. The amount of these smoked cats found in standing stone structures in the British Isles and north-central Europe "suggest[s] a possible

Anglo-Saxon or Norse origin for the custom" (ibid.). In Germany, archaeologists have recorded almost one hundred of these poor kitties. There were even seventeen found in Australia, with many more expected worldwide.

Although there was skepticism about whether these cats were intentionally mummified and entombed in buildings, archaeologists more often find that the cats in these burials are pinned or tied in various poses, along with rodents or birds positioned as if they were in the "midst of an attack or chase, or positioned with their prey in their mouths" (Sheehan, 1990). There is some disagreement as to whether these cats were buried alive, but it seems more likely that they were buried after death.

Unlike witch bottles, research into the ritual concealment of cats in buildings is often overlooked, even though there have been nearly forty cases of dried cats identified in US buildings in the Mid-Atlantic region. Workers renovating the Ohio Statehouse found a shoebox dating to the nineteenth century that contained the skeletal remains of a cat behind the plaster wall in the cupola at the top of the rotunda. The difficulty reaching the location indicates it was clearly a deliberate act (Manning, 2014). One theory for this practice is that it was a way to ward off vermin, as a sort of sympathetic magic. This theory makes some sense considering the fact that numerous cats were posed in aggressive postures, often with prey. However, some archaeologists argue this may have been a ritual sacrifice to the building in exchange for structural safety.

Vampire of Venice

Francesco was pensive, grateful that the morning sun felt warm on his weary face. The young *monatti*, or corpse carrier, was exhausted from his unending labors. He and his brothers worked with hundreds of other young men who appeared to resist the latest outbreak of plague in his beloved Republic of Venice. Returning Holy Roman soldiers brought the disease back from their involvement in the Thirty Years' War. By 1630, nearly five hundred Venetians perished every day. The plague would go on to claim one-third of the republic's citizens. Strong, healthy young men like Francesco were employed to undertake the never-ending tasks of removing bodies and digging mass graves. That morning's burden was different, however. On that morning, Francesco was ordered to exhume the body of an old heathen woman who had succumbed just two months earlier. He was to verify that this lost soul was truly dead—and that it had stayed dead.

In life, this woman was not from Venice. Perhaps she was originally from the Ottoman lands to the east, near present-day Turkey or Syria. As she fell ill, she was sequestered to Lazzaretto Vecchio, the quarantine island in Venice's central lagoon. The conditions at the hospital there were hellish and even worse for the poor, immigrants, and those who did not know Christ. This woman died without baptism, and when her cadaver was thrown onto the cart to be moved to Lazzaretto Nuovo, the island of final internment, a friar who oversaw the operation declared her to be a shroud eater, a hideous type of ghoulish vampire. She was buried with a brick jammed so tightly in her mouth that it nearly dislocated her jaw, then marked for later exhumation.

When Francesco and his younger brother, Pietro, finally removed the last shovelfuls of earth, they were aghast. The friar's suspicions proved correct. The corpse appeared to have moved since it was originally buried, but the brick seemed to have prevented it from feeding upon the bodies of other plague victims. The brothers set about reburying the vampire.

Pre-Enlightenment gravediggers who reopened mass graves would often encounter horrid corpses that exhibited signs of life after death. Bloated bodies, hair and nails that continued to grow, and mouths, noses, and eyes that seeped dark fluids led the superstitious to believe that they had witnessed signs of the undead. In some cases, the shrouds that covered the faces of the deceased would have decayed due to bacteria present in the mouths to reveal the gruesome teeth and receding gums associated with vampirism. These creatures were known as "shroud eaters."

In 2006, the sixteenth-century remains of the "Vampire of Venice" were discovered entombed on a small island approximately two miles northeast of the city. The skeleton, with a brick firmly lodged in its mouth, was found in a mass grave that dates to 1576. It marks the first archaeological discovery that demonstrates the ritual exorcism of a vampire.

Frozen Inca Mummies

In 1996, at the top of the glacier-covered volcano Sara Sara in southwest Peru, between Laguna Parinacocha and the Río Ocoña, the body of a fifteen-year-old girl was found. She froze to death after she was left as a sacrifice to the gods. Three years later, archaeologists discovered three more frozen child sacrifices (two girls and one boy estimated to be eight to fourteen years old), just below the top of the summit of Volcán Llullaillaco in northwestern Argentina. These Inca children had been fattened, adored, and drugged, before priests left them on the summit to die.

Archaeologists from all over the world were interested in studying these sacrificed children, as their bodies were some of the most well-preserved mummies ever found. The mummies do not appear to be dehydrated. The body fluids and almost complete organs can provide a wealth of data on eating habits, illnesses, and more. The skin and organs are still intact, and in one case, the heart is still filled with frozen blood. They looked as though they had simply fallen asleep, yet they were about five hundred years old. As such, researchers were able to perform numerous tests on the bodies and the array of pristine artifacts that were left with them as offerings.

Researchers refer to the children as the Lightning Girl, Maiden of Llullaillaco, and The Boy. The Lightning Girl's name is in reference to the fact that her body had been burned after being struck by lightning after her death. She was six years old at the time of her death. The Lightning Girl's skull was elongated, and she was dressed in a light brown dress and wrapped in a yellow and red blanket. The Boy was about seven years old at the time of his death, which appears to have been a traumatic event, as he had vomit and blood on his clothes. The Boy also had dislocated bones and was the only one of the children who was restrained. His skull was lightly elongated, and he was wearing a gray tunic, silver jewelry, and wrapped in a brown and red blanket. Due to his restraints, it is believed he was suffocated. The Maiden of Llullaillaco was an *aclla*, or Sun Virgin, a chosen woman who was selected at ten years old and sent to live with other chosen girls who were taken from their families and made to live with priests in preparation for their futures as wives of noblemen, priestesses, and sacrifices.

Researchers started their analysis on the hair of the mummies, which can be regarded as a chemical diary about the last months of their lives. The conclusion was that the children's diet suddenly changed twelve months before their death. The Maiden of Llullaillaco had the longest hair at almost ten inches long. Because it had been braided, then grew out, researchers were able to determine that she was chosen for sacrifice about a year before death. Further analysis showed that her diet consisted of barley, meat, and potatoes, which is evident from the nitrogen and carbon in her hair. However, a year before her death, she suddenly ate a lot of llama meat and corn, which were luxury foods. Then, in the six months leading to her death, she was made to consume coca and chicha alcohol (a fermented maize beer). This may have been a way to subdue her so that she would not object or struggle against her fate.

Other markers in their hair indicate height changes, leading researcher to hypothesize that the children were taken from poor farming families and cared for as high-status people before being sacrificed to the gods. Similar changes were observed with the other two children. Aside from the injuries on The Boy, the bodies were unharmed at the time of sacrifice, which may mean that rather than a violent death, they froze or died of altitude sickness. Still, this was an unimaginably horrific fate.

CHAPTER 11

Deliver Us from Evil

Horrific human sacrifices, cathedrals of human remains, horned humanoids, and modern-day murderers who invoke Sumerian demons by moonlight: these are all dreadful realities of human history, both ancient and modern. However, the question remains: Are demons *real?* Is evil a cultural construct, or can it be measured using scientific methods and tools? On our quest to find the truth behind demons, it is becoming apparent that they are not real in a tangible sense. To date, there have been no verified discoveries of demon skeletal remains. Although there have been unusual remains found, many of them have not been closely examined, or when they are, they are proven to be a hoax. Now, there are ways to scientifically test these extraordinary finds.

Body of Proof

Like the peat bog workers near the village of Yde in 1897, people often report finding demon bodies. Until now, the technology to determine what these bodies really were did not exist. Thus, folktales and legends ran wild, twisting and changing with every person through which they passed. Take for instance the mystery of the "Nazi demon skulls" found in remote in a cave on Mount Bolshoi Tjach, Russia. In 2014, two strange skulls were discovered in a forest close to a site where a Nazi briefcase was found. With the briefcase was a map dated to 1941. The briefcase had the SS Ahnenerbe insignia on it. The SS Ahnenerbe was a secret Nazi archaeological research organization led by Heinrich Himmler. Members of the SS Ahnenerbe were an elite group of archaeologists and scientists who were hired to look for information on human origins, Aryan race theory, occultism, UFOlogy, and the paranormal. Given how close these skulls were to the Nazi artifacts, as well as the site's remoteness, people have speculated that the Nazis could have used this area to summon demons.

As for the two unusual skulls, researchers have claimed they belong to neither animal nor human. The skulls are quite bizarre in appearance. They indeed resemble demons, as they have what appear to be a large humanoid face with huge eye sockets and two symmetrical protrusions from which there are two branches in the form of horns. Additionally, the facial bone is flat. As someone who has studied osteoarchaeology, I can say that from the photos I have personally seen, they are certainly bone and not an intentional hoax. However, there are many natural reasons for bone to deform whether when the organism was alive or after death. Photos of the demon skulls were sent to paleontologists in Moscow. Although they admitted that they had never seen anything like this before, they postulated that it was the skull of a ram that had been trapped in a river for a long time and succumbed to erosion, which caused drastic changes to its structure and shape. The only way to know for certain is to perform a DNA analysis, but no such analysis is planned.

Atacama Alien

About a decade ago, a bizarre little skeleton dubbed "Ata" was discovered in the Atacama Desert in Chile. It is about six inches long and has an odd conical head and only ten ribs. Some thought it was the remains of a primate, and others speculated that it was an extraterrestrial or even a devil. A proper scientific investigation into Ata began in 2012 when professor Gary Nolan, one of the authors of the initial research paper about Ata, received a call from a friend who thought he had discovered an "alien." However, research published in the scientific journal *Genome Research* claims scientists have successfully mapped the genome of Ata and can thereby conclude with certainty that the remains are those of a human being with many genetic birth defects such as dwarfism, scoliosis, and others relating specifically to muscle and bone deformation (Bhattacharya et al., 2018). Additionally, it confirmed her sex as female with both South American and European ancestry, which leads researchers to believe her body may be newer than five hundred years and links her European ancestry to sometime after the pre-Columbian period. Although her bones were that of a six-year-old, scientists believe this was a result of one of her bone deformities and not indicative of her age upon dying. Ata is probably not that old either; based on the intact state of her skeleton, they believe she was a baby who died during or shortly after birth. Researchers intend to study Ata even further in the hopes they will find out more about her disorders and gain new insights that may help patients now. They eventually intend to return little Ata to Chile, so that she may be buried with respect.

Rotating Egyptian Statue

At the Manchester Museum in Britain, a ten-inch ancient Egyptian statue dating from around 1800 BCE was seen and even recorded moving on its own. The statue of Neb-Senu was found in a tomb next to a mummy. She performed the role of a kind of offering to one of the main gods of the ancient Egyptian pantheon, Osiris. Every night, the statue would move unassisted. Every day, workers would find that the statue had rotated 180 degrees without anyone's help. The staff would move the statue back where it belonged, but still they would find it turned and facing the wrong direction.

The museum decided to set up video surveillance to see if they could solve this mystery, but to their surprise, they found that the figure, which stands behind a window of glass, did indeed move by itself. The video footage has gone viral and can be found online on a number of platforms. When asked to explain, the curator said, "In ancient Egypt they believed that if the mummy is destroyed then the statuette can act as an alternative vessel for the spirit" (Legge and Price, 2013). The hieroglyphics on the back of the tomb where the statue was discovered asked for bread, beer, and meat, presumably in case it came to life. Perhaps that's why the statue moved? It was possessed by the spirit that once inhabited the mummy?

After more thoughtful analysis, including using paranormal tools like the ones Mike Ricksecker discussed, the curator determined that there was a small convex bump on the bottom of the statue that would cause it to move in response to the rumbles from the buses and traffic outside, as well as the footsteps of the passing visitors. The curator affixed a conservation-grade film on the bottom off the artifact so that it can no longer move. Problem solved.

Curse of the Pharaohs

Highclere Castle, known to some only as the set of *Downton Abbey*, has an interesting connection to the Pharaoh's Curse. It was the ancestral home of the fifth Earl of Carnarvon, a man who would pave the way to modern Egyptology, and in so doing, pay a hefty price. Lord Carnarvon traveled to Egypt for the first time in 1909. He was weakened by a serious car accident, and his doctor advised that the damp English climate was bad for his health. So, like so many wealthy gentlemen of his era, he spent the winter in warm Egypt. There, he discovered his passion for ancient civilizations and became involved in archaeological excavations.

A few years later, he met Howard Carter. Carter had come to Egypt in 1891 when he was only seventeen years old. He worked as a draftsman for the Egypt Exploration Fund and eventually worked his way up to the inspector general of the Upper Egyptian Antiquities Administration. Things did not go smoothly for Carter, though. A fight broke out between him and some drunken French tourists. When Carter was told he needed to apologize for his misconduct, he simply quit his job instead.

Carter began working as an artist, an antiques dealer, and tour guide until he met Lord Carnarvon. They became friends right away, as they both shared a love for Egyptian history. From 1909 on, Carter was financially supported by the wealthy lord in his excavations. Carter made a few archaeological discoveries, but the biggest one was yet to come. November 4, 1922, he made the discovery of his life: the almost untouched tomb of

Tutankhamun. The site was crammed with so many archaeological treasures that Howard Carter was only able to say wonderful things, in an urgent message to Lord Carnarvon, who had just arrived from England.

Strange things happened on the day of the opening of the tomb, like the cobra that killed Howard Carter's canary. Interestingly enough, the cobra was a symbol of the pharaohs. A few months later, a mosquito in Cairo bit Lord Carnarvon. It became infected, as his immune system was so weakened that he got pneumonia. In a feverish delirium he screamed over and over that a bird was scratching his face (Booth, 2009). Weakened by blood poisoning and an infection, he died at night in his hotel room on April 5, 1923. At the same time, all the lights in Cairo went out, and his dog Susie also died at the manor house in Hampshire. Strangely, doctors who later examined the body of Tutankhamun found that he had a black spot on his left cheek in the exact same spot where Carnarvon had been bitten by the mosquito. Yet, the curse does not end with Carnarvon's death:

- Lord Carnarvon's half-brother, Aubrey Herbert, died of peritonitis.

- Professor Lafleur who studied the found treasures suddenly died.

- Archaeologist Hugh Evelyn-White fell into depression and hanged himself in 1924. His suicide note read, "I have succumbed to a curse which forces me to disappear" (Lace, 2008).

- The scientist who X-rayed the mummy, Douglas Reed, suddenly died.

- Egyptian prince Ali Fahmy Bey was murdered in a hotel in London, and his brother committed suicide.

- Papyrus expert Bernard Grenfell and Egyptologist Aaron Ember died in 1926.

- The right hand of Howard Carter, Arthur Mace, died five years after Lord Carnarvon. He suffered from symptoms that resembled an arsenic poisoning.

- In 1929, the wife of Lord Carnarvon died.

- Richard Bethell, who was responsible for cataloging the found treasures, died in 1929 at the age of thirty-five.

- In 1930, Richard Bethell's father committed suicide by jumping out of the window of his apartment in London. In his bedroom he had a vase from the tomb of Tutankhamun.

- Shocked by the number of deaths, a government official was sent to the grave to investigate the situation. He also became ill within a few days and died.

- In total, seventeen people who can be directly or indirectly associated with the tomb of Tutankhamun died unnatural, strange, or early deaths within a few years.

- Oddly enough, the ultimate discoverer of the grave, Howard Carter, remained outside. He eventually died in March of 1939 of natural causes.

Was a curse to blame for all of these deaths? Some speculate that the ancient Egyptians had some sort of radioactive medium on the walls of the tombs designed to harm tomb raiders if the tomb was ever disturbed. Or perhaps there was a virus lurking in the unsealed tomb? Was it just too much for Carnarvon's weak immune system?

Modern research has shown that ancient mummies can harbor two potentially dangerous types of molds, *Aspergillus niger* and *Aspergillus flavus,* and their tomb walls can have bacteria like *Staphylococcus* and *Pseudomonas.* If someone were to breathe these in, it could cause a range of nasty upper respiratory symptoms and even death. If that were not enough, Egyptian tombs can contain gases left over from the embalming process. Things such hydrogen sulfide, ammonia gas, and formaldehyde can cause severe respiratory distress and, in some cases, also death.

There is an old joke about archaeology, that when you blow your nose after a long day in the field, you blow out dirt. Well, according to Kenneth Feder, professor of archaeology at Central Connecticut State University in New Britain and coeditor of the book *Dangerous Places: Health, Safety, and Archaeology,* "Clearly you have been breathing it in, and if you have been exposed to molds, spores, or fungi that lay dormant in the earth, there is at least a possibility of being exposed to some nasty stuff" (Poirier and Feder, 2001).

By opening these tombs that have been sealed off for potentially thousands of years, archaeologists and even looters can unknowingly expose themselves to countless dangers. Again, science has proven that there is a logical explanation behind the Pharaoh's Curse. This surely explains Carnarvon's death, as he had an already weakened immune system. Still, it does not explain the other deaths. Maybe there is something to the curse after all!

Too Afraid

In the early twentieth century, the Pharaoh's Curse caused a media sensation. This was the heyday of archaeology, when the discipline was still relatively new and the criteria were far different for who could be an archaeologist and what systems were necessary to do archaeology. This does not mean that explorers and others did not see the value in unearthing history's most valuable secrets. However, before the organization and legitimization of archaeology as a field of inquiry, artifacts were handled in a way consistent with the beliefs and understanding of whoever happened to find them. This has led to the loss of countless treasures, the likes of which we may never know. Many lost artifacts have become part of someone's private collection or been damaged, destroyed, intentionally defaced, or even reburied, as was the case with the Aztec statue of Coatlicue. This tremendous, ten-foot-tall basalt statue was found once, reburied, found again, and then reburied—all because it was considered evil and frightening!

In 1790, archaeologists uncovered the massive Aztec goddess of childbirth under the Zócalo, an important Aztec site in Mexico City. The intimidating figure now towers over visitors in Mexico City's National Museum of Anthropology. It is believed that the statue had already been found during the Spanish Conquest, but it was buried because those who uncovered it thought it was too frightening and possibly possessed. Chronicled in 1792, pioneering archaeologist and astronomer Antonio de León y Gama described two of his most important discoveries, the Aztec calendar stone and the statue of Coatlicue. In opposition to authors of previous centuries, Gama praised Aztec society and their scientific and artistic achievements in his book, which also featured watercolor drawings. Thanks to the publication of the book, many consider León y Gama as the first Mexican archaeologist. However, in his book, he mistakenly thought the statue depicted Teoyaomiqui, the Aztec flower god. Yet again though, as if to add insult to injury, the statue was reburied because the archaeologists believed it was too frightening and too pagan. It was later rediscovered in the twentieth century and properly researched and curated. Now, Coatlicue is one of the most important and famous (perhaps infamous) representations of Aztec art and culture. Who was Coatlicue, and why would this statue be so horrifying?

Coatlicue is an Aztec goddess of childbirth. There are many versions of her myths, but they all share the same story of how Coatlicue was impregnated with the sun god. Most of them are also consistent in what followed: the birth of another god, and the angry daughter planned to kill everyone. In the myths, Coatlicue was a goddess at a shrine located on a sacred and legendary mountain called Coatepec. As she swept the floor of the shrine, she noticed a ball of feathers that was floating down from the sky. Entranced, she followed its movement, caught it, and placed it in her belt. She later found out that the ball of feathers had somehow impregnated her. Her child was Huitzilopochtli, god of the sun.

Coatlicue already had a daughter, the goddess Coyolxauhqui. Coyolxauhqui was furious that her mother was pregnant, so she planned to kill her and her unborn child. She amassed an army and marched to the mountain. Someone, possibly the sympathetic son of Coatlicue, leaked the word of the battle. This made Coatlicue immensely frightened, and she prepared to go without a fight, but Huitzilopochtli told her not to worry. When Coyolxauhqui and her army reached the mountain, Coyolxauhqui charged at her mother. At that moment, Huitzilopochtli sprang from the womb fully grown, adorned in armor and carrying a sword. He sliced

Coyolxauhqui's head off and threw her off the mountain. It is said that as her body fell, came apart in pieces, and was scattered to the wind. Coyolxauhqui's head was thrown into the air and became the moon, and her army became the stars. The whole point of this myth is to show how the sun always triumphs over the moon and stars. Coatlicue was safe. Later in life, she gave birth to the well-known god Quetzalcoatl. Coatlicue gave birth to many other gods, which earned her the name Teteoinnan, or "mother of the gods."

With Coatlicue's violent nature and imposing figure, it would have been easy for early Christian explorers to view her as a demon. An analysis of the statue shows how visually rich their interpretation of Coatlicue's story was. The claws on Coatlicue's feet are there so that she can tear apart her food, which was human flesh. Because of this, Coatlicue is also associated with star demons, the Tzitzimime. The Aztecs thought that if the sun ever failed to rise or there were a solar eclipse, Coatlicue and the Tzitzimime would descend to the Earth and eat most, if not all, of humankind in their anger.

What did this statue look like that made it so frightening? First, the skirt is made of snakes, and what looks at first glance like her head is actually two snakes facing each other. Coatlicue's name literally means "Skirt of Snakes." At the top of the statue are two snake heads. Their eyes, teeth, underbellies, and even tongues look as though they form a face, but the Coatlicue statue is headless. A few myths in Aztec culture may explain this, such as Coatlicue sacrificing herself to make the universe or being beheaded when she gave birth to the sun god, Huitzilopochtli.

Coatlicue, Museo Nacional de Antropología.

Looking at the upper torso and chest, Coatlicue is wearing a necklace made of human hands and hearts. Also, her arms are in a predatory/strike position, and she is leaning forward slightly, which amplifies the scary effect. The necklace covers most of her breasts, which are described as growing large because of all of the children she had. Her stomach has rolls, another sign she has been pregnant. Her belt consists of two snake bodies. The belt buckle of the snake belt is a human skull, and tassels that are snake heads dangle directly below it. The skirt, the main part of this statue and Coatlicue's namesake, shows intertwined snakes that graze the goddess's feet. The feet have claws and also eyes that stare upward. This statue may be horrific, but it is expertly carved. It is a true testament to the artistic abilities and craftsmanship of Aztec culture.

Scientific Demonology

In Morocco, scientists have been studying the science behind spirit possession since the 1990s. Their theory is that certain diseases define certain afflictions as the penetration of demonic spirit into the human body in a physical mechanism comparable to that of microbes. It is like a "germ theory" of demonology. This molecular explanation for demons is currently under investigation and is opening the door to the possibility of a scientific explanation, beyond mental illness, to confirm the existence of evil entities. In Morocco, in the Islamic system, jinn, or evil spirits, are a central element to epilepsy, autoimmune disorders, and many other afflictions (Dieste, 2014).

According to some of the Muslim scientists working on this research, evil spirits are invisible to the naked eye, just like microbes. They contend that the existence of these evil spirit molecules does not depend on human perception. However, they claim to be getting closer to identifying them using advanced microscopy (Sharāwĭ, 2001). The researchers theorize that the molecular composition of evil spirits makes them averse to light, explaining why they often appear at night or in the dark. They have their own special physical laws and life cycles, and can rapidly multiple after entering our bloodstream (ibid.). Scientists have even been devising mathematic formulas to calculate their movement and behavior (Dieste, 2014).

Should science dictate our beliefs, or should our beliefs dictate our science? This is still a question that some have difficulty answering. Within the skeptical philosophy, the existence of an objective reality is denied. The concept of reality is regarded by this school of thought as no more than a subjective mental construct. Cognitive awareness allows us to distinguish between reality and fantasy. Fantasy and imagination spring from the individual emotional world. However, fantasy and imagination can reach beyond the individual perception through art, literature, and all that archaeologists call artifacts—things made by human beings that are of cultural or historical interest. Einstein wrote:

> The belief in an external world independent of the
> perceiving subject is the basis of all natural science.
> Since, however, sense perception only gives information
> of this external world or of physical reality indirectly,
> we can only grasp the latter by speculative means. It
> follows from this that our notions of physical reality can
> never be final. We must always be ready to change these
> notions—that is to say, the axiomatic basis of physics—
> in order to do justice to perceived facts in the most
> perfect way. (Schilpp, 1970)

It is on this premise that we seek meaning and realness outside of ourselves. Whether we will find it is perhaps the ultimate mystery.

CHAPTER 12

May We No Longer Fear Any Evil

The name of this chapter comes from the last few lines of the Catholic rite of exorcism. It acts as a reminder that fear is what weakens us in the face of evil, and it is courage that we need to face our demons. Courage is not the absence of fear, but rather the willingness to persist in spite of it. Our search for the truth about demons has brought us from the ochre-stained caves of prehistory to the blood-stained floors of a modern crime scene. Along the way, we have explored different customs and beliefs of a diverse range of cultures. Certainly, this was not a complete study of all the world's interpretations of and beliefs about demons, possession, or sinister relics. To do so would be futile because history is brimming with demons and evil, whether real or imagined. When looking at the role demons played in the development of civilization, it becomes clear that demons may have served as a linguistic tool for both understanding and communicating concepts of specific ways of suffering.

In the prehistoric caves of Europe, chimeras adorn the walls. These early demons were symbols containing increasingly complex ideas relating to health, pain, suffering, and healing. The same can be said for the thousands of artifacts and sites discovered around the world that depict human suffering. If we expand our ideas and understanding of how evil manifests in the lives of humans, perhaps we will better understand what we can do in our daily lives to protect ourselves from everyday forms of evil.

Knowledge Is Power

How do we know if demons are real? Whether or not demons are real may just depend on your interpretation of the word "real." To the mothers of Pazuzu Algarad's victims, demons may very well be real. The demon in this case took the form of a flesh-and-blood human being. Algarad's invocations and offerings opened a doorway to evil and allowed him to become the embodiment of the Pazuzu spirit. Likewise, the flesh-and-blood sacrifices and invocations in the Pawnee Morning Star Ceremony were believed to be required for a warrior to embody the Morning Star. With so many belief systems and individualized perspectives, whether demons are real may only depend on your own personal concept of reality.

To question the realness of something seems a bit pedantic, as though it is clear whether something is real or not. According to proto-Enlightenment philosopher and occultist Francis Bacon (January 1561–April 1626) science is a "uniquely structured reasoning system based on inductive logic" (Vanpool and Vanpool, 1999). In many scientific disciplines, reality is therefore assumed to be self-evident; in philosophy and philosophy of science, however, the concept of "reality" is more problematic.

Earlier science and philosophy operated under the assumption that humans can acquire rock-solid, true, and absolute knowledge of the world that surrounds us. We would come to understand that this knowledge corresponds to a reality. This would lead us to what the Greek philosophers called *nous,* meaning "the intellect, or reasoning, needed to understand the ultimate truth or reality." According to Plato, there was a reality behind the sensory world. He called that reality the theory of Forms. He reasoned that there are eternal and unchangeable models of various phenomena that we encounter in nature. For example: Cookies are baked in a bakery. No cookie is identical, but they still look alike. They have a common origin; all cookies are shaped according to the same cookie cutter.

As Plato concludes, reality has two parts. The first part is the sensory world. From this, we can only get a rough or incomplete knowledge by using our senses. Even if we have scientific tools, they still depend on our observation. Everything in the sensory world flows and is therefore not eternal. We can only have vague reflections of ideas about what we observe. Only things that we recognize with our minds can be certain. For example, the sum of the angles of a triangle will always be 180 degrees. Plato also states that all phenomena in nature are only shadows of eternal forms or ideas.

The philosopher Immanuel Kant, however, was the first to make a distinction between the world as such, independent of human perception and the human. Kant emphasized that it cannot be shown that the knowledge we hold about the world relates directly to that world. Kant argued that time and space were not properties of the world, but that they are relative to the human experience. Time and space are human perception of the world.

Kant now stated more generally that man cannot know the "world in itself." With this, Kant took a critical view of the possibility of ever knowing truth. Kant believed that knowledge cannot be considered absolute truth. Absolute truth could only be judged by its correctness, effectiveness, and provability through empirical science. Therefore, knowledge of reality is not possible, only probable, at best. Here, however, a distinction can be made between formal, transcendent knowledge as contained in mathematics or in logic and empirical, practical, scientific knowledge. Can demons hold up to this form of reasoning? Throughout the beginning chapters, we saw how the concept of "demonizing" out-of-favor deities is a subjective, cultural, and, arguably, a linguistic construct. In chapter 11, we explored some claims about physical demons, all of which could not be proven, or were disproven, using science. Does this mean demons do *not* exist?

The Metaphysics of Demons

First, the word "demon" is derived from the Greek word *daemon*, which is essentially an inner spirit, or an *inspired* entity that occupies the reality between the divine and the mortal. In the classical sense, a demon does is not necessarily evil. This corresponds with how most people through history have viewed demons. Although they can be evil, they can also serve a purpose, as King Solomon learned by commanding the demons to build his temple. Given the manner with which this word is used, we can also state that demons are nonhuman. We cannot determine that demons are wandering human souls, extraterrestrial life-forms, interdimensional beings, or otherwise. At least, not with the tools we have now. As Arthur C. Clarke so famously said, "Any sufficiently advanced technology is indistinguishable from magic." Could demons be such advanced beings that some humans have simply relegated them to the realm of fantasy? As previously discussed, scientific studies are underway all over the world to test theories pertaining to the physical nature of demons. Perhaps demons are like germ theory. Perhaps our current state of technology will not yet allow us to observe them.

According to the archaeological record, historic texts, and the current beliefs of a variety of faiths, there do seem to be some interesting consistent characteristics shared by demons. For example, demons are believed not to be human. They operate in a physical reality or dimension unknown to us through science. Demons often live in connection with natural forces. This is a result of their being bound to higher universal force. A demon can also interact with and affect the physical world. They use these abilities to physically manifest power to garner a reaction from humans. When someone does indeed react, especially with fear, the demon identifies a potential for weakness in the person. Demons feed off these reactions, as they have been described as "psychic vampires" by multiple cultures going back four thousand years.

To understand what demons are, it is necessary to have some insight into duality, the opposition between light and dark, and the function of evil in the universe. As incarnate beings who live in duality, we could not grow psychologically and spiritually without the existence of darkness or evil. Without the dark, we would not recognize the light. Without fear and hatred, we would not really know security and love. If we were to experience only positivity, we would have nothing with which to compare the negative aspects of our existence. Metaphysically speaking, duality exists so that souls can grow in consciousness and become awakened, enlightened, and empowered cocreators. In short, the dark has an important function in the multiverse. Our history is in duality, but human consciousness has the power to transcend duality. By understanding the myths of demons and their role in mythic thought, we can fully understand the function demons play in both the ancient and modern world. To understand, we must first address what is meant by "myth."

It is commonly accepted that myth was a tool for ancient people to explain the unexplainable. However, this interpretation is not entirely true and gives insufficient credit to our amazing ancestors. Hence, I argue that myth is not the search for meaning. Meaning is a product of the rational mind; it is the Logos, or logical part of the consciousness, that seeks to make connections between events and experiences. To entertain Jaynes's theory once more, this rational mind resides in the right hemisphere, whereas the left hemisphere applies language, symbols, and provides our inner voice. It makes the narrative between our internal world and external world.

These are some metaphysical and philosophical ways to explore the "realness" of demons. A more esoteric approach to challenging our perceptions of what is real is to consider the thoughtform, or *tulpa*, from both Buddhist philosophy and Western occultism.

Thoughtforms

Inspired by the Buddhist *tulpa*, or astral body, Western occult traditions reimagined these into thoughtforms. The term "thoughtform" was used in 1927 in the Theosophist translation of the *Tibetan Book of the Dead* to describe a thought that has materialized or attained a physical form only by the power of a human mind: one only has to believe enough to conjure an actual entity. Theosophists divided thoughtforms into three categories:

1. An image of the thinker himself, where it seems that person is in two places at once.

2. An image of a physical object linked to the thought.

3. An independent image that expresses the inherent qualities of the conscious thought.

Like Solomon summoning jinn to help build his temple, thoughtforms could be conjured to help with a variety of things. According to the Tibetan occultists, thoughtforms can happen almost automatically if the will is strong enough. For obvious reasons, this could be dangerous because if you conjure or create a thoughtform and stop using it, it does not just automatically go away. The idea is that you have to consciously make it disappear. Thoughtforms can even survive their creators and turn up in their next lives, and it has been said that it is not always a pleasant reunion. It is therefore important to understand what a thoughtform is.

British occultist Aleister Crowley (October 1875–1947), dubbed "the wickedest man in the world," always thought he had the power to manifest anything he desired. Crowley decided he desired a position as the new leader of the occult organization Hermetic Order of the Golden Dawn. However, the order seemed to reject his idea. Crowley became so angry that he determined that S. L. MacGregor Mathers, one of his rivals, had psychically attacked him. So, Crowley did what you would expect from the wickedest man in the world. He summoned Beelzebub and his demons to retaliate.

Mathers had planned for the attack by creating a vampiric thoughtform by channeling the power of Mars. Once the thoughtform materialized, he sent it to attack Crowley, but something went terribly wrong for Mathers. Crowley was a much more skillful occultist, so he took the thoughtform over and sent it back to Mathers, only this time, the entity was far more depraved. According to legend, this thoughtform feud went on for a number of years. Journalists all around the world reported on the feud. Mathers died in 1918 (some say because of the attacks), but he left his account of what the thoughtform supposedly looked like, describing the thoughtform as a female with no visible lower body. It had deep glowing eyes, a flat head, and tiny flippers for arms, as though they had not been fully formed. He described all of the limbs as appearing in a fetal stage. Perhaps worse was its long, gray tongue, described as hollow and tube-like. The thoughtform would use its spindly tongue to try to suck the life out of Mathers and eventually succeeded.

How would one make a thoughtform? According to modern theosophical and metaphysical tradition, to make a thoughtform, you would first have to have a physical vessel for the entity. This object would be linked to your intention: a heart for love, a statue of an eagle for freedom, and so on. The vessel would be purified or blessed, then placed in front of the conjurer as they meditated. During meditation, they would visualize a sphere of light above their head. This visualizing would continue until the conjurer would see the light travel from inside the head to the outside before finally resting on the spot between the eyebrows, often identified as sixth chakra, *ajna* in Sanskrit. This is known as the seat of "concealed wisdom." Once the light is there, an intense concentration is needed to focus the conjurer's own intention. By projecting their intention, and concentrating, the image of the thoughtform is supposed to begin taking form.

At this point, the conjuring can begin to see the thoughtform clearly in their mind's eye. This supposedly takes a great deal of concentration, as well as controlled breathing. Similar to Yoga, the conjurer would be instructed to breathe in deeply with their mouth and breathe out through their nose quickly, pulling their stomach in and holding their breath for a count of three. After continued concentration and controlled breathing, the conjurer would blow their breath over the blessed vessel, all the while still visualizing and focusing their energy onto the image of the thoughtform that they have contrived. This transference of breath is believed to carry a life force wherein their intentions are now magically transferred into the vessel and continue to vibrate with the energy of their wish.

Finally, the conjurer would give their thoughtform a name that is relevant to the work that it will do. They would say that name aloud and tell the thoughtform what to do and when, where, how long, and also when to stop. Dabbling in this sort of work is not recommended, especially if one is not a trained occultist. If someone tries to conjure a thoughtform, they may be opening themselves up to untold dangers, which is why trained occultists also have ways to destroy their own thoughtforms. Killing a thoughtform is a lot more difficult than creating one, especially if it has been allowed to age. As soon as the thoughtform is created, with a physical or a spiritual form, it is believed that the entity begins to build up memories. If a certain form of consciousness is added, it will try to "survive." Thus, to kill their thoughtform, the conjurer must pour water and soil from the vessel into a well in the garden or hold it under water completely, until they are able to feel the thoughtform dissolve and fade away. At this point, the conjurer would conclude by declaring out loud that the connection has been broken and that the thoughtform is now dead.

Thoughtforms may sound easy to dismiss as a story from a bygone era, but since about 2009, some believe that a new thoughtform has taken shape. Its name is Slenderman. Some believe Slenderman to be an ancient creature who has manifested in different cultures throughout different periods of history. His most recent manifestation has been online in varying forums. According to researcher Nick Redfern, "More and more people are following, and arguably even worshiping and devoting their lives to, the Slenderman as he becomes ever stronger and more physical in our world" (Redfern, 2018). There have indeed been news reports of this entity encouraging children and young people to do horrific things. Could Slenderman be a thoughtform, or simply another evil folk demon, only this time high tech? Can believing in something enough bring it to life?

Maybe to believe in something enough is to be inspired. From the Latin *inspirare,* meaning "to breathe or blow into," the word "inspired" originally described the experience of a supernatural being imparting an idea to someone. Although demons may not be tangible, or arguably even real, could just the belief be enough to inspire someone to carry out evil acts in the name of a demon? In some ways, then, demons can be very real to some people, which can have lasting and real consequences.

How to Protect Yourself

In the midst of all we've explored, we are left with an overarching question: If evil entities are real, how can we protect ourselves from their corrupt influence? Historically, people have tried various methods to protect themselves from evil, including rituals, spells, herbs, tokens, amulets, and even bottles of urine. Contemporary exorcists seem to agree on some basic methods to keep safe from malevolent forces. As the exorcist Bill Bean said, you need to be vigilant and stay in warrior mode.

Identify the Demon

- Try to learn the name of the demon, but be on guard and skeptical. Even if you think it is a demonic entity you are encountering, it may also be something natural and explainable.

- Look for unusual mood swings. Demons like to tease and mock their victim. They will not fully manifest until they know that there is a weakness or vulnerability to exploit. Also, if your quiet, peaceful home suddenly becomes chaotic, maybe you should take a second look.

- Look for activities generally associated with poltergeists, such as moving furniture, flying objects, or electrical disturbances. Demons are powerful, but they need to absorb a large amount of energy in order to display terrifying phenomena like throwing objects or levitation.

- Be aware of unusual sounds and smells. Demons may be recorded on camera or with audio recording devices. You may see strange orbs in the background of your photos. Additionally, demons will leave a terrible smell described as that of rotten meat or sulfur.

Defense Against Demons

- Clean your personal spaces and living environment. If your home, office, or even car is a mess, it creates a dirty, unpleasant environment that can attract a demon. Build your spiritual protection by surrounding yourself with positive reminders of faith, family, and friends. Remove any objects that cause too much negativity or bad feelings. Listen to your gut.

- Prepare an area in your home that creates a spiritual atmosphere with whatever makes you feel a sense of connection, such as incense, candles, crystals, and so on.

- Do not underestimate demons, and do not try to engage in dialogue.

- Defend yourself against demons by reciting prayers or meditations. It will help you feel centered and calm, and it has been reported to repel demons.

If You Think You Are Possessed

If you do believe you are possessed, the very first thing you want to do is contact a mental health professional. This is not to imply that it is all in your head. The truth is that a trusted mental health professional can actually put you in touch with a credible exorcist. There are even mental health professionals who are, themselves, exorcists. In addition to the help they may be able to provide in finding an exorcist in your area and faith, they will be able to give you the initial assessment that will be needed before an exorcism is granted. Although you may feel uncomfortable reaching out to a mental health professional for something spiritual, remember that the field of psychology deals with understanding the psyche, which is the Latin translation of the Greek word for the human soul, mind, or spirit.

One very important thing to remember above all else: Many faiths and traditions teach that the ultimate goal of a demon is to steal your soul and cause your ultimate demise. If you feel that you cannot take it anymore and have thoughts of hurting yourself or others, please do not be afraid to call the National Suicide Prevention Lifeline at 1-800-273-8255. The Lifeline provides free, twenty-four-hour confidential support for anyone in distress, and prevention and crisis resources for you or your loved ones. There is even a confidential chat at *www.suicidepreventionlifeline.org.*

Go in Peace

The takeaway here is simple: Do not be afraid. Second, there does not appear to be enough evidence to prove any benefits to using amulets, charms, crosses, or any other tangible material object that may promise to protect you from demonic forces. However, there is also not enough, if any, evidence to show that they are harmful.

The third point is to be aware of your own well-being so that you do not become easy prey of negative energy, no matter what shape it may take. Live fully and consciously, and always try to be aware of any negative self-talk so that you can replace it with positive affirmations. Live a purpose-driven life. Make sure that everything you do has value in your own eyes, not others. Unplug from the Internet for a bit. Get outside in nature and reconnect to the world.

The fourth point is also relatively simple. Allow your inner light to shine. Try doing things that bring about positive changes in yourself and others. One of the best ways to manifest positive change is through volunteering your time to a charitable cause. Not only will it allow you to let your light shine for others, you will benefit from making meaningful human connections. When we are isolated, it is easy to feel weak, fearful, or vulnerable.

To be in "warrior mode," as Bill Bean would say, we must train like warriors. We must strengthen both our physical and spiritual bodies. Therefore, we must keep our bodies healthy and clean. Even the ancients knew that the body is a temple, so it must be treated accordingly.

So, live cheerfully and do not worry about not being taken seriously. Many people believe that they must maintain a detached attitude or a hard exterior in order to appear strong. The truth is, those people are often the weakest, and most vulnerable. You can be intelligent, serious, and mature, and still live with a sense of cheer. Remember that cheerfulness is not the same as frivolity. Cheerfulness is born of a fighting spirit. Frivolity is just a manifestation of cowardly escape.

But that does not mean that a confrontation with the dark is always easy. To put it simply, evil is the absence of love, compassion, joy, warmth, acceptance, peace, and light. Evil is not the same as the human emotions that we tend to reject, such as anger. Anger is a normal human feeling, and a psychologically mature person can handle such a powerfully charged human emotion. Evil is different. The absence of love and light can teach us to be a light in the darkness ourselves and a source of love for others. Pain and trauma caused by malicious acts can teach us about the deepest forms of healing. In short, all manifestations of evil can teach us to grow in spiritual mastery, integrity, responsibility, and wisdom.

What is evil archaeology? People recognize evil it when they encounter it. Many of the sites and artifacts explored in this book may seem evil upon first impression, but when studying them in greater detail, you will find that some of this is not evil at all. In archaeology, one of the most important concepts is context, the position of an artifact or site in time and space. Context includes the analysis of how an archaeological find got there and what has happened to it since. It is very easy to become focused on sites and relics and to miss the broader relevance of the discovery with regard to human history and culture. Without context, sites like Stonehenge or Göbekli Tepe become a pile of rocks. Without context, Pazuzu figures and bearded satyrs start to look like cartoon characters. Perhaps what evil archaeology can teach us about human history and culture is that the evil we see in sinister relics is really just a reflection of the evil we fear in ourselves.

Afterword

I'd be remiss if I didn't admit to some of the strange and unsettling experiences that I had while writing this book. Allow me to first say that I do not consider myself a very religious person. I was raised Catholic, attended Catholic school, and observed all the traditions (in some cases, superstitions) that entails. I left the Catholic faith and spent years traveling the country and studying various faith traditions and beliefs. I interviewed many people, explored ancient sites and texts, and experienced diverse forms of worship. After many years searching, I found that my personal faith is situated in the Anglican tradition. Thus, I identify as a Christian. This is not to suggest that I only believe the doctrine of this tradition, but rather, my faith allows me to continue to explore alternative interpretations of the Scripture.

A bishop once told me, all truth can be found in Christianity. Now, this at first can be interpreted as denying all things outside of the Christian faith, but that would be incorrect. In the Anglican faith, it means something altogether more inclusive. According to the Reverend Dr. Dennis Maynard, Anglican philosophy comes from a variety of areas including science, art, literature, poetry, history, and other religions because Anglicans "do not see ourselves in opposition to any field of inquiry, but in concert with it" (Maynard, 1994). Hence, I can maintain a connection to the Christian tradition while I still seek higher truths in science, history, art, and philosophy. While I continue seeking, I am at peace with my personal relationship to the higher power.

That said, when I announced that I would be writing a book on evil, curses, demons, and possessions, many friends and colleagues expressed their concern. Collectively, they feared that by focusing so much energy on evil, I would be vulnerable to negative forces. I had people say they would pray for me, burn sage, cast spells, you name it. I found it all a bit superstitious and, in some ways, admittedly silly. I mean, how would I be vulnerable to anything simply by researching and writing? Nevertheless, I graciously accepted their kindness and thanked them for their concern, but I wasn't the least bit afraid.

As I began collecting research, it was as though sources just magically appeared wherever I looked. For instance, on the day I first decided to do this book, I was in a thrift store hunting for any discarded antiques, an activity I like to call "retail archaeology." As I combed over the mismatched teacups, I caught a glimpse of a slightly tattered black book open and facedown on the floor. It was *The Encyclopedia of Witchcraft & Demonology* by Rossell Hope Robbins, printed in 1959. It seemed like it was just lying there, waiting for me to find it. What a lucky find! That wasn't all. A series of lucky things started happening to me, one by one. So much for bad luck or negative forces!

As I got deeper into writing, I noticed my luck started to change. It started with a sudden and unexplainable heart problem. I was in a research library one afternoon, looking through archives, when my heart started racing. I was trembling all over, then fell to the floor. The librarian called an ambulance, and I was taken to a local hospital with my heart beating at peak beats per minute. The hospital released me later that evening with no explanation, only a referral to a cardiologist. A week later, I was at another library studying scans of sixteenth-century Devil's pacts when the very same thing happened. This time, I managed to drive myself to the emergency room. Again, I was released with no explanation. These "attacks" started to come with increasing frequency, always when I was working. Then, the nightmares started. Every night, I was haunted with dreams about very specific demons. I attributed it to all of the research into spooky old documents and dusty primary sources.

I began to wake up in the middle of the night trembling, my room freezing cold. My heart was beating through the roof. I wondered, could these be panic attacks? After consulting my physician, he assured me that they were not panic attacks, then he referred me to heart specialist. After seeing multiple specialists at the Cleveland Clinic, the cardiologists told me my heart was perfectly healthy, which came as no surprise as I am what most would consider a "health nut." I eat a plant-based diet, jog, play tennis, and have no family history of heart disease. Plus, I was still only in my mid-thirties. If it was not my heart, then what was the problem? After seeing an electrophysiologist, he informed me that "something" was interfering with the electrical pathways of my heart. When asked what, he said he didn't know and that nobody did. I received so many second opinions, all of which reached the same diagnosis: sudden onset of inappropriate sinus tachycardia. It is a tachycardia (fast heart rate) coming from the sinus node of the heart. They call it "inappropriate" because they cannot find an appropriate trigger for these attacks.

This diagnosis took many months to reach. During those months, I tried to power through completing this book, but it seemed like one thing after another stood in my way; everything from small day-to-day hurdles to major challenges. For instance, while I was working late one night finishing a chapter, the electricity in my house surged so badly, that an outlet burst into flames, igniting a stack of *National Geographic* magazines I had nearby. Had I been asleep, my whole house would have gone up in flames.

As a naturally optimistic and determined person, I am not usually fazed by much. Then came the sudden death of my cat Bailey, whom I lovingly referred to as my research assistant because he was always stepping on my laptop keys, inserting such "interesting" prose as "ujjjjjjjjjjjjjjjjjjjjj." Throughout the writing of this book, Bailey kept getting weaker and unexplainably ill. I took him to three different veterinarians, all of whom did not know what to do for Bailey. The night I finished this book, Bailey collapsed. He died the next morning, leaving me sick with grief for the loss of my little friend of so many years.

As I mentioned, I am not a superstitious person, but if I were, I would say that there was some sort of connection, not just because some unfortunate events occurred, but because of the energy I felt. I have never experienced anything like it before. It seemed as though the more time I spent engaging my mind in the realm of demons, the worse I felt both physically and spiritually. This was particularly strange because before I started, I felt certain that this would be one of my favorite projects. I mean, it sounded so fun and interesting. Why was the entire process almost debilitating? Why did everything seem to go back to relatively normal as soon as I finished the book?

I could not help but to reflect on my past experiences in South Carolina, my exchange with Paula, and my discussion will Bill, the exorcist. A friend of mine who is a psychic medium suggested that perhaps a negative entity had attached itself to the old demonology book I brought home from the thrift store. She also theorized that this entity may have somehow "jumped" from the book to my poor cat, as sort of a scapegoat. This is clearly a lot of speculation. Nevertheless, she insisted on burning sage in my home office and blessing the area where I write as a precaution. These are just personal reflections. As with most of the human experience, our perceptions are subjective, and we are prone to making connections. We may secretly hope that by making connections between the events and experiences in our lives, we will someday see the meaning in it all. There may likely never be answers, certainly none that could be studied scientifically. So, I will just leave it there for you to make of it what you will.

Bibliography

Annus, Amar, and Alan Lenzi. *Ludlul Bēl Nēmeqi: The Standard Babylonian Poem of the Righteous Sufferer*. Helsinki: Neo-Assyrian Text Corpus Project, 2010.

Arnott, Robert, Stanley Finger, and C. U. M. Smith. *Trepanation: History, Discovery, Theory*. Boca Raton, FL: CRC Press, 2014.

Austin, Jon. "Mystery of the 'Alien Skulls' and Nazi Briefcase Found in Remote Mountain Woods." *Daily Express*, January 16, 2016. *https://www.express.co.uk/news/science/634733/Do-demon-skulls-and-Nazi-briefcase-discoveries-prove-Third-Reich-contacted-ALIENS*.

Ball, K. "The Devil's Pact: Diabolic Writing and Oral Tradition." *Western Folklore* 73, no. 4 (September 2014): 385–409. *https://une.idm.oclc.org/login?url=https://search-proquest-com.une.idm.oclc.org/docview/1666795905?accountid=12756*.

Bamberger, Avigail Manekin. "An Akkadian Demon in the Talmud: Between Šulak and Bar-Širiqa 1." *Journal for the Study of Judaism* 44, no. 2 (2013): 282–87. doi:10.1163/15700631-12340381.

Berg, Bruce L., and Howard Lune. *Qualitative Research Methods for the Social Sciences*. Harlow, Essex: Pearson, 2014.

Bhattacharya, Sanchita, Jian Li, Alexandra Sockell, Matthew J. Kan, Felice A. Bava, Shann-Ching Chen, María C. Ávila-Arcos, Xuhuai Ji, Emery Smith, Narges B. Asadi, Ralph S. Lachman, Hugo Y. K. Lam, Carlos D. Bustamante, Atul J.

Butte, and Garry P. Nolan. "Whole-genome Sequencing of Atacama Skeleton Shows Novel Mutations Linked with Dysplasia." *Genome Research* 28, no. 4 (2018): 423–31. doi:10.1101/gr.223693.117.

Black, Joseph. *The Broadview Anthology of British Literature.* Peterborough: Broadview Press, 2011.

Blatty, William Peter. *The Exorcist.* New York: Bantam Books, 1974.

Bober, Phyllis Fray. "Cernunnos: Origin and Transformation of a Celtic Divinity." *American Journal of Archaeology* 55, no. 1 (1951): 13. doi:10.2307/501179.

Booth, Charlotte. *The Curse of the Mummy: And Other Mysteries of Ancient Egypt.* Richmond, VA: Oneworld, 2009.

Brandolini, Simona. "A Volte Tornano. Restituiti a Pompei Tanti Reperti Trafugati." *La Corriere Della Sera,* October 13, 2015. *https://corrieredelmezzogiorno.corriere.it/napoli/cronaca/15_ottobre_13/tornano-pompei-centinaia-reperti-trafugati-anni-d5f1e53e-7175-11e5-8a35-85b57ae5d6f8.shtml.*

Brinkley, Bill. "Priest Frees Mt. Rainier Boy Reported Held in Devil's Grip." *Washington Post,* August 20, 1949.

Buren, E. Douglas van. "New Evidence Concerning an Eye-Divinity." *Iraq* 17, no. 2 (1955): 164. doi:10.2307/4241726.

Burstyn, Ellen. *Lessons in Becoming Myself.* New York: Riverhead Books, 2006.

Caesar, Julius. Translated by W. A. MacDevitt. *The Conquest of Gaul.* New York: Digireads, 2012.

Campbell, Joseph, Bill D. Moyers, and Betty S. Flowers. *The Power of Myth.* N.p.: Turtleback Books, 2012.

Carmichael, James. *King James the First, Daemonologie (1597): Newes from Scotland, Declaring the Damnable Life and Death of Doctor Fian, a Notable Sorcerer Who Was Burned at Edenbrough in Ianuary Last (1591)*. 1597. https://www.bl.uk/collection-items/witchcraft-pamphlet-news-from-scotland-1591.

Carroll-Koch, Laura. "The Brain, Our Silent Partner: Anatomy and Cognition." Lecture, New Haven, CT. December 03, 2002.

Carus, Paul. *Open Court*. Chicago: Open Court, 1887.

C.C.M. "More Luciferian Phenomena." *Light: A Journal of Psychical, Occult, and Mystical Research* 15 (October 12, 1895): 49–96.

Clower, William T., and Stanley Finger. "Discovering Trepanation: The Contribution of Paul Broca." *Neurosurgery* 49, no. 6 (2001): 1417–426. doi:10.1097/00006123-200112000-00021.

Conway, Moncure Daniel. *Human Sacrifices in England*. London, 1876.

Craffert, Pieter F. *The Life of a Galilean Shaman: Jesus of Nazareth in Anthropological-historical Perspective*. Eugene, OR: Cascade Books, 2008.

Davis, James A., Tom W. Smith, and Peter V. Marsden. "General Social Surveys, 1972–2006 [Cumulative File]." *ICPSR Data Holdings*, 2007. doi:10.3886/icpsr04697.

"The Devil in the Convent." *The American Historical Review* 107, no. 5 (December 20, 2002): 1379–411. doi:10.1086/ahr/107.5.1379.

Dewhurst, Kenneth, and A. W. Beard. "Sudden Religious Conversions in Temporal Lobe Epilepsy." *Epilepsy & Behavior* 4, no. 1 (1970): 78–87. doi:10.1016/s1525-5050(02)00688-1.

Dieste, Josep Lluís Mateo. "'Spirits Are Like Microbes': Islamic Revival and the Definition of Morality in Moroccan Exorcism." *Contemporary Islam* 9, no. 1 (2014): 45–63. doi:10.1007/s11562-014-0312-0.

Dods, Marcus. *The City of God.* Edinburgh, Scotland: T. & T. Clark, 1878.

Donnelly, Mark P., and Daniel Diehl. *The Big Book of Pain: Torture & Punishment Through History.* Charleston, SC: History Press, 2012.

Dunlap, Rhodes. "King James and Some Witches: The Date and Text of the Daemonologie." *Philological Quarterly* 54, no. 1 (Winter 1975): 40-47.

French, Chris. "Pope Francis and the Psychology of Exorcism and Possession." *The Guardian.* July 09, 2014. *https://www.theguardian.com/science/2014/jul/09/pope-francis-psychology-exorcism-possession.*

Galenos. Translated by P. N. Singer. *Galen: Selected Works.* Oxford, UK: Oxford University Press, 1997.

Garinet, Jules. *Histoire de la Magie en France, Depuis le Commencement de la Monarchie Jusquà Nos Jours.* Paris: Foulon et Cie., 1818.

Germond, Philippe. *Sekhmet et la Protection du Monde.* Basel, Switzerland: Ägyptologisches Seminar der Universität Basel, 1982.

Gornstein, Leslie. "A Jinx in a Box?" *Los Angeles Times,* July 25, 2004. *http://articles.latimes.com/2004/jul/25/entertainment/ca-gornstein25.*

Hall, Manly Palmer. *Initiates of the Flame.* Los Angeles, CA: Phoenix Press, 1934.

Handwerk, Branden. "Egypt's 'King Tut Curse' Caused by Tomb Toxins?" *National Geographic.* May 6, 2005. *https://news. nationalgeographic.com/news/2005/05/0506_050506_ mummycurse.html.*

Hertz, Robert. *Death and the Right Hand.* London, UK: Routledge, 2008.

Jaquith, James R. "Florentine Codex: General History of the Things of New Spain. Arthur J. O. Anderson, Charles E. Dibble." *American Anthropologist* 85, no. 2 (1983): 486–87. doi:10.1525/aa.1983.85.2.02a00760.

Jastrow, Morris. *Aspects of Religious Belief and Practice in Babylonia and Assyria.* New York: Knickerbocker Press, 1911.

Jaynes, Julian. *The Origin of Consciousness in the Breakdown of the Bicameral Mind.* Boston: Houghton Mifflin, 2003.

Jones, Lindsay, and Mircea Eliade. *Encyclopedia of Religion.* Detroit: Macmillan Reference, 2005.

Klingender, F. D. *Animals in Art and Thought: To the End of the Middle Ages.* London: Routledge and K. Paul, 1971.

Kotzé, Zacharias. "The Evil Eye of Sumerian Deities." *Asian and African Studies* 26, no. 1 (2017): 102–15. doi:13351257.

Lace, William W. *The Curse of King Tut.* San Diego, CA: ReferencePoint Press, 2008.

Lea, Henry Charles. *A History of the Inquisition of the Middle Ages.* New York: Harper & Brothers, 1888.

Legge, James, and Campbell Price. "Riddle of Rotating Egyptian Statue in Manchester Museum Solved." *The Independent.* November 21, 2013. *https://www.independent.co.uk/news/uk/ home-news/mystery-solved-manchester-museums-spinning- ancient-egyptian-statue-isnt-cursed-8951201.html.*

Linton, Ralph. "The Origin of the Skidi Pawnee Sacrifice to the Morning Star." *American Anthropologist* 28, no. 3 (1926): 457–66. doi:10.1525/aa.1926.28.3.02a00010.

Mackey, Albert Gallatin. *A Lexicon of Freemasonry*. London: Richard Griffen and Co., 1857.

Manning, M. Chris. "The Material Culture of Ritual Concealments in the United States." *Historical Archaeology* 48, no. 3 (2014): 52–83. doi:10.1007/bf03376937.

Maynard, Dennis R. *Those Episkopols*. N.p.: Dionysus Publications, 1994.

McCown, Chester C. *The Testament of Solomon*. Chicago: University of Chicago, 1915.

Menotti, Francesco, and Aidan O'Sullivan. *The Oxford Handbook of Wetland Archaeology*. Oxford: Oxford University Press, 2013.

Milton, John, and Anna Baldwin. *Paradise Lost*. Oxford, England: Oxford University Press, 2008.

Osungbade, Kayode O., and Sunday L. Siyanbade. "Myths, Misconceptions, and Misunderstandings About Epilepsy in a Nigerian Rural Community: Implications for Community Health Interventions." *Epilepsy & Behavior* 21, no. 4 (2011): 425–29. doi:10.1016/j.yebeh.2011.05.014.

Pike, Albert. *Morals and Dogma*. New York: Macoy Pub. & Masonic Supply, 1900.

Plutarch, Frank Cole, and Harold F. Babbitt, et al. Plutarch's Moralia. Cambridge, MA: Harvard University Press, 2005.

Poirier, David A., and Kenneth L. Feder. *Dangerous Places: Health, Safety, and Archaeology*. Westport, CT: Bergin & Garvey, 2001.

Redfern, Nick. *Slenderman Mysteries: An Internet Urban Legend Comes to Life.* Wayne, NJ: Career Press, 2018.

Robben, Antonius C .G. M. *Death, Mourning, and Burial: A Cross-cultural Reader.* Malden, MA: Blackwell, 2012.

Roughead, W. "Scottish Witch Trials: The Witches of North Berwick." *Juridical Review* 25, no. 2 (1913): 161–84. doi:0022-6785.

Rudwin, Maximilian J. *The Devil in Legend and Literature.* La Salle, IL: Open Court, 1973.

Sabbath, Roberta Sterman. *Sacred Tropes: Tanakh, New Testament, and Quran as Literature and Culture.* Leiden, The Netherlands: Brill, 2009.

Schilpp, Paul Arthur. *Albert Einstein, Philosopher-Scientist.* La Salle, IL: Open Court, 1970.

Scurlock, JoAnn. *Magico-medical Means of Treating Ghost-induced Illness in Ancient Mesopotamia.* Leiden, The Netherlands: Brill Styx, 2006.

Shakespeare, William. *The Complete Works of William Shakespeare.* New York: Barnes & Noble, 2015.

Sharāwī, Muḥammad Mutawallī. *The End of the World.* London: Dar Al Taqwa, 2001.

Sheehan, John. "A Seventeenth Century Dried Cat from Ennis Friary." *North Munster Antiquarian Journal* 32 (1990): 64–69.

Starr Miller Paget, Edith. *Occult Theocrasy.* New York: Imprimerie F. Paillart, 1933.

Stewart, Alan. *The Cradle King: A Life of James VI and I.* London: Pimlico, 2003.

Stol, Marten. *Epilepsy in Babylonia*. Groningen, The Netherlands: Styx, 1993.

Strickland, Debra Higgs. *Saracens, Demons and Jews: Making Monsters in Medieval Art*. New Jersey: Princeton University Press, 2003.

Thompson, Campbell. "Assyrian Medical Texts: From the Originals in the British Museum." *Nature* 114, no. 2854 (1924): 48. doi:10.1038/114048c0.

Vanpool, Christine S., and Todd L. Vanpool. "The Scientific Nature of Postprocessualism." *American Antiquity* 64, no. 1 (1999): 33–53. doi:10.2307/2694344.

Waite, Arthur Edward, and R. A. Gilbert. *Devil-worship in France, with Diana Vaughan and the Question of Modern Palladism*. Boston, MA: Weiser Books, 2003.

Wakefield, E. G., and S. C. Dellinger. "Possible Reasons for Trephining the Skull in the Past." *Ciba Symposium* 1 (1939): 166–69.

"What Is Cognitive Archaeology?" *Cambridge Archaeological Journal* 3, no. 02 (1993): 247. doi:10.1017/s095977430000086x.

About the Author

Dr. Heather Lynn is an author, historian, and renegade archaeologist on a quest to uncover the truth behind ancient mysteries. After earning her associate degree in archaeology, she continued to study anthropology and history, earning her Master of Arts in history. Her thesis examined the intersection of class inequality, consumer culture, propaganda, and public education in early modern Europe. She went on to pursue her doctorate in education at the University of New England. She is a lifelong learner and holds certificates in human osteoarchaeology from Leiden University, archeoastronomy from Politecnico di Milano.

Heather is a member of professional organizations including the American Historical Association, the Society for Historical Archaeology (SHA), Association of Ancient Historians, and the World Archaeological Congress. Her research includes hidden history, ancient mysteries, mythology, folklore, the occult, symbolism, paleocontact, and consciousness. In addition to regular appearances on radio programs like *Coast to Coast AM*, Heather has been a historical consultant for television programs, including History Channel's *Ancient Aliens*. She also speaks at various conferences and events. Her own show, *Digging Deeper*, is now available on YouTube, iTunes, TuneIn, Stitcher, and Spotify.

Website: *www.drheatherlynn.com*